He Alone

BY DOROTHY SUN AND PATRICIA STONE TAYLOR

Published by

Christian Aid Books
a division of

Christian Aid Mission
1201 Fifth Street
Charlottesville, VA 22902

www.christianaid.org

ISBN 978-1-940545-13-4

Christian Aid Books

Printed in the USA

Acknowledgments

Mrs. Patricia Taylor—I was fully blessed by my chief editor, mind reader, soul mate and sweet gifted sister-in-Christ, Patricia. Without her labor, and the unbelievably beautiful words she has put in my book, especially because of the way she loves me and encourages me, this book could not have been done. I thank God for you, dear sister, having your support and making this book possible.

I want to give special thanks to the leaders and my sweet supportive coworkers at Christian Aid Mission. They all love me, giving me opportunities to serve and helping me in many ways. Without their support, I could not have finished this book.

My family, husband, twin sons and grandchildren were also a part of my being able to write this book. They understood the extra time I needed to concentrate. With mission trips, speaking at churches, office work, and caring for my sick husband, time I might have spent with them was limited. When my twin sons' families had special need of my help, they didn't let me know. Sometimes, however, when I needed a break from my busy life, I got to spend time with my grandchildren, who make my life more interesting, more fun, with both laughter and comforting. That helped me to finish this book.

I want to thank Robert Hodgson, my mother's godson, who really knows my roots. I appreciate his love, gentleness, kindness, humility, and humor. The true story of the relationship between my parents, my family and him, shows the compassion between the ordinary American Christian and Chinese Christian family.

I want to give special thanks to the following dear ones, friends and donors who prayed for and supported the writing of my story, through my highs and my lows: faithful servants of God, Dr. and Rev. Thomas Wang and Dr. Yeou-cherng Bor, Mr. and Mrs. Jim and Nela Wright, and their company F.H.G., and his family. Mr. and Mrs. Greg and Carolyn Phillips, Rev. and Mrs. Bob and Lowana Atkins, Miss Mary Frances Boys and Miss Elaine Eckel, Miss Wendy Tang, Mr. and Mrs. Daniel and Charmaine Mao, the Raleigh Chinese Christian Church in N.C. and Intercede International, Canada. Also, in Taiwan, Mr. Gary Liu, Mr. and Mrs. Steve and Shi Feng Chang, Mr. and Mrs. Hank M. H. Du, Executive Director of World Vision in Taiwan; Pastor and Mrs. Yun Guang Shi of Bread Life Christian Church in Taipei; Hsin-Chu International Church; Elder Mrs. Ming Fong and Ping Chen of Taipei Nan King East Road Christian Church; Rev. Caleb and Mrs. Ong, the pastor of Tainan Assembly of God; Mr. and Mrs. James and Joan Shia, the General Director and all the staff of Chinese Christian Evangelistic Association (CCEA) .

All the blessings of the Lord given to me abundantly through all of them will be remembered in heaven.

Table of Contents

Preface

My reasons for writing this second book are simple but important. Readers of my first book, **_Clay in the Potter's Hand_**, have asked what happened next in my life. This book will answer those questions. Telling what the Lord has done for me can prove the only God, the Son of God, the Holy Spirit is the God of all nations. This God is the only one true and living God. Anyone who believes in Him can have intimacy with Him. He alone has the ability to change our lives and to grow us past our expectations and limitations to glorify His name.   —Dorothy Sun

Working with Dorothy has been a joy as well as a learning experience. Her story is compelling, funny in places, even whimsical in others. Tears fall freely as terrible wartime memories surface, but always there is the knowledge that God knew where Dorothy was at all times. Loving her, carrying her and bringing her safely through, He alone is responsible for her life unfolding in such a way that she has this story to tell. His amazing grace, abounding love and power to heal, to teach about forgiveness, and to give others hope...whether they are in prison, at home, at work, in despair... shows us we have reason to rejoice despite our circumstances.

I pray that the many stories shared in this book will show you how God can completely transform a life. The situations Dorothy has lived through make me marvel at her endurance, joy, and survival ability. We have the same Savior and love of life despite the sometimes difficult circumstances God has allowed in our lives. I truly thank God for her friendship and example of running the race to the finish.   —Patricia Stone Taylor

"Having known Dorothy Sun over the course of nearly 28 years, from her first days at Christian Aid Mission, I have personally seen her dedication to the Lord, and her heartfelt desire to bring others into His flock. Dorothy's cheerful and enthusiastic nature comes through as she tells of amazing, often miraculous, ways God has used her to show that He truly is with us no matter what happens. May this, her second book, delight you with Dorothy's true stories demonstrating how God can use a life to bring glory to His name. Over many thousands of miles, Dorothy has journeyed throughout China and many other lands sharing the Gospel message of God's love and care. Travel with her as you read and learn how the Master works and can bring good out of any situation when you love, trust, and depend upon the Living God."

—Cynthia Finley
President of Christian Aid Mission
Charlottesville, Virginia

Foreward

He Alone is a book you will not be able to put down easily once you get started. From the beginning to the end, the author's extraordinary life story will captivate your attention, inspire your curiosity and whet your appetite. In almost every turn of events, you find yourself asking the question, "What happens next?"

Dorothy Sun, born of devout Christian parents in China in the 1930s, lived through a time of national upheaval, political struggle and social transformation. Her real-life experiences during those tumultuous years have forged her will to survive, kept her faith in Jesus Christ and emboldened her tenacity to witness for her Lord regardless of circumstances!

You will enjoy and indeed be enthralled in reading different episodes of her unusual life, which include:

• Happy early childhood with parents in China.

• Life under Japanese invasion of China.

• Grateful memories of generous help and "Rescuers" from America, including the Flying Tigers volunteer air force under the direction of General Claire Chennault.

• Fond memories of her dear father David Chang, a faithful servant of God, who suffered greatly under both Japanese occupation and Communist rule.

• On account of her Christian faith and under false accusation, she was imprisoned for 20 years in hard labor camp.

• Spiritual lessons she learned through sufferings: "God dealt with my pride. I was proud of my humility and my willingness to suffer for the Lord. The hard labor camp was my seminary training."

• Happy marriage with Freddie Sun and their ministry with China Aid Mission, serving in China and beyond.

• On August 22, 2012, God called home her beloved Freddie, her life-companion and co-laborer. Under this great loss, Dorothy declared, "with Freddie gone, I worked twice as hard".

• In view of the moral deterioration of today's China, she felt a calling of God to initiate a ministry to pre-school children, to nurture China's toddlers between ages 2 to 5 on basic morality and faith, before any human ideologies invade their young minds.

May this book, *He Alone*, be widely read and digested by brothers and sisters both east and west. And may the Lord speak through the testimony of His handmaid Dorothy to inspire Christians around the world for sanctified living and evangelistic outreach. Amen!

> Dr. Thomas Wang
> President Emeritus
> Great Commission Center International

Foreward

From Brokenness to Blessing—Only in Him, through Him, and by Him

The story goes like this. Michelangelo carved the statue David out of a piece of marble that had been rejected by other sculptors, who believed the marble was unworthy of an attempt. An admirer asked Michelangelo how he crafted this masterpiece of form and beauty. Michelangelo offered a strikingly simple answer: all that he had to do was to chip away all of the parts that weren't David. And so, gradually, tap by tap, David emerged. The secret of Michelangelo's sculpting was that he had a laser-sharp vision, seeing through the amorphous mass of rock to its ultimate form. He created through what he negated. Michelangelo knew David. And God knows us!

In one of the lectures that he delivered, apologist Ravi Zacharias eloquently quoted the following words:

'When God wants to drill a man,
  and thrill a man, and skill a man,
When God wants to mold a man
  to play the noblest part,
When He yearns with all His heart
  to create so great and bold a man,
That all the world should be amazed,
Watch His methods, watch His ways:
How he ruthlessly perfects
  whom He royally elects;
How he hammers him and hurts him,
And with mighty blows converts him
  into shapes and forms of clay
Which only God can understand,
While man's tortured heart is crying

and he lifts beseeching hands;
Yet God bends but never breaks
  when man's good He undertakes,
How He uses
  whom he chooses,
And with mighty power infuses him,
With every act induces him
  to try his splendor out,
God knows what he's about…'

In her book *He Alone* Dorothy emphatically conveys to her readers that "when God wants to mold a man… and bold a man… watch his methods, watch His ways…:" She is like that piece slab of raw marble. With a precision of vision, God looked inside the marble and saw "David" in her. And He used sufferings and trials as the chisel to chip away those that did not belong to her so that God can conform and transform her to His Son's image (Romans 8:29). Because of the Lord's great love and his never-failing compassion, "God bends but never breaks." Those are His methods, those are His ways.

Across history, God calls ordinary people like Dorothy—with all her weakness, yet her great devotion to God—who, molded by God, became extraordinary beings. God has deliberately and with profound wisdom chosen her so that He might gloriously change her and display her before the whole world as one of the holy examples of His handiwork. God reveals to us how an ordinary life lived out faithfully to the calling can impact the eternal destiny of an untold number of people, even a nation. Through brokenness Dorothy became God's workmanship, created beautifully and wonderfully in Christ Jesus. Equipped for all kinds of good works, she brought blessings to this world that God so loved. The life of Dorothy is evidence of just such inspired transformation. So it was for Dorothy, so it is for us. Her story is ours.

Dorothy loves music, especially classical music. Dorothy's life is like an oratorio. When conducted by God, the greatest composer and conductor of the universe, it displays in front of us one of the most glorious melodies and ingenious harmonies that not only touches our heart, fills our mind, but also resonates in our soul. Interestingly enough, one of her favorite pieces is Messiah, composed by George Frederic Handel. There is a story told of Handel, upon completing the "Hallelujah" chorus, he turned to his servant with tears in his eyes. "I did think I did see all Heaven before me, and the great God Himself," he cried. Realizing that the music had not come from his creative abilities, at the end of his manuscript he wrote the inscription: S.D.G.—Soli Deo Gloria, to signify the work was for God's glory "only."

Hence, the title of this book: "He Alone."

I pray that this book will motivate you, as it does me, to re-evaluate your priority in life; that it will mobilize you to re-engage this world with the Gospel of Jesus Christ; and that it will move you to recommit to a lifestyle that everything that is done is for God's glory.

> Soli Deo Gloria!
> Dr. Yeou-cherng Bor
> Chairman, Board of Directors,
> Ambassador for Christ
> Charlottesville, Virginia

◆ HE ALONE ◆

Chapter I

The Voice in the Clouds

A clear memory from when I was four years old is that voice in the clouds. After my afternoon nap, my nanny often allowed me to go into the front yard to enjoy a quiet time. I had a hiding place under the locust tree surrounded by lilacs and wisteria where I sat on a small stool. Those beautiful clouds gave my imagination flight. I saw flowers, rabbits, pretty girls, an angel with a trumpet, snow-covered mountains, white boats on a blue sea. These things created fantasies and I made up silly stories. Some were happy, some sad, some scary, some beautiful. It passed the time for me until my parents came home from work. I felt protected there in my special place, hidden from my ten-year-old brother, Joe, who often played mean tricks on me.

When Mom and Dad came home I could not tell my daddy how Joe had pushed me around. My mom forbade me to tell daddy even though she knew that Joe had been mean to me. There was a problem of jealousy between us which my mother did not want to make worse. My brother Caleb, two years older than Joe, was nice to me. Joe had his piano lessons and both boys had homework to do, so Mom was busy with the servants and helping the boys with their homework.

Whenever my father was home, I was like his shadow. I loved putting my small hand in his big, soft, fat hand. It made me feel loved and safe. I loved watching him work at his big, long walnut desk. It was a precious place for me to sit. At that time he was doing work on "God's wonderful revelation in Chinese Characters." I was his sole audience, student and fan. What an amazing time it was when he discovered certain pictographic characters precisely revealing the Bible stories. He was so excited, he jumped up and walked around the room with his arms lifted up, praising the Lord. I jumped down from the desk and followed him around as I clapped my hands. What a happy time it was!

Once, late in the day as I was waiting for my daddy to come home, I was fearful of my naughty brother, Joe, poking fun at me again. I felt so lonely and afraid. My heart murmured, "Daddy, come back, Daddy, please come back!" As my tired eyes kept watching through the rosy glow of the clouds in the sunset, I heard a clear and gentle voice, like music through the clouds, "Child, I am your daddy. I am here with you every day," the voice said. I wondered and cried out aloud, "Jesus, is that you?" The voice slowly disappeared with the cool breeze and the beautiful clouds. "Ye-..ye-s..." Even though I was disappointed the voice was gone, the gentle words behind the clouds remained deeply sealed in my heart forever. I knew then and now, "Oh, I love you Jesus. You are my daddy, too."

As my life continued and I grew older, the Scripture gave me the answer why and how the Lord Jesus knew me and loved me when I was little: *"Before I formed you in the womb I knew you, before you were born I set you apart"* (Jeremiah 1:5a); and (Psalm 22:9) *"Yet you brought me out of the womb; you made me trust in you even at my mother's breast."* I still love to watch the clouds moving and changing as I make up my stories. They are always my companions, even now.

That day long ago I told my parents and all my brothers and my older sister and my nanny about the gentle voice in the clouds. My daddy replied to me, "When you were in Mom's womb we had dedicated you to our Lord as a tribute, because He gave me a wife like an angel, a Proverbs 31 woman." At bedtime Mom sang, "His eyes are on the sparrow and I know He watches me" as a lullaby.

When I was four months old, I suffered from pneumonia. I had a very high fever for ten days and no treatments could help me. It was in the days before antibiotics. I was in a coma and breathing heavily and twisting every which way. The doctors thought I would not survive, as my parents prayed fervently for me.

God answers prayer always. A friend of my family visited us unexpectedly. He was a famous traditional Chinese medical doctor. Immediately he used Chinese herbal soups and snatched my life back. One week later, I was totally healed. My mom said, "Child, our Jesus is watching over you and loves you more than we do. Remember you are His."

My naughty brother, Joe, however, continued to bully me. I prayed to my daddy, Jesus, "Please stop Joe from bullying me. Please give him a time out!" I believed that the Lord Jesus is my daddy, too. Our Lord Jesus listened to my prayer. He can make a way, always, even when there seems to be no way.

Joe started to be more interested in music. He played the piano more than four hours every day, voluntarily and beautifully. My mom sent him to a Russian piano teacher. Joe made rapid progress with his piano lessons. He did well on his recitals and received prizes for his good work. His teacher was so proud of him remarking that Joe was a very promising, talented youth. That gave Joe more pride, causing him to double his efforts to improve himself constantly. So I discovered that Joe paid more attention to showing a gentlemanly, professional manner. With school, the concerts, and piano practice, Joe was busy enough with his own affairs. He no longer had time to bother me. Our Joe really changed a lot. I enjoyed his piano concerts very much, even becoming his fan. Thank you, Lord Jesus, for giving me a musician brother, Joe.

◆ HE ALONE ◆

Chapter II

My Baptism

By 1944 the Japanese had already invaded and occupied China for seven long years. The Japanese used the "Three Alls Policy" toward the Chinese - essentially it was: kill them all, burn them all and plunder them all. They not only occupied our territory but also snatched our abundant resources, priceless national treasures, historic relics and the people's property and valuables. They even grabbed Chinese rice, providing it only to their soldiers. Chinese were forbidden to have any.

My own eyes witnessed the extremely dreadful tragic scenes in which Japanese soldiers were horribly cruel and inhumane. My brother and my father were arrested and put into jail for not cooperating with the Japanese. They had horrible experiences of brutal torture. We were not allowed to learn any foreign languages at school except for Japanese. Instead of broadcasting a variety of music, only Japanese operas were played. Martial law ordered blackouts every evening to deter the Chinese and American airplanes from bombing Japanese military installations, munitions and arsenals. What a dark and gruesome world it was at that time. As an antidote, I often noticed Mom and Dad turn the radio very low in order to hear short wave news on the Chongching channel, that city being the center of Chinese government resisting Japanese aggression.

Before the Japanese sneak attack on Pearl Harbor, the news we heard from short waves all were sad ones. Nazi Germany kept madly and brutally invading many countries in Europe, murdered millions of innocent people and the Jews in particular. For their part, the Japanese cruelly invaded and occupied China and South East Asia. Millions upon millions of Chinese national military, as well as those of the United Kingdom, the United States, France, and Russia had their troops and people die in a bloody violent war of resisting Japanese and Nazi aggression. That came to be known as World War II.

After U.S. President Roosevelt declared war against the Japanese and Nazi Germany, the Allied Nations (U.K, U.S., France, China, and Russia) military forces were united and intensified rapidly. Especially after the D-Day landing counter attack, the news from short waves was more and more exciting in victorious events. I can see my parents clapping their hands and whispering, "Hail, US army! Thank God! Alleluia! " Even though I was just eight years old, I loved clapping my hands and shouting with them. My mother quickly covered my mouth as she said, "God answered our prayers, but only when His time comes and we will see His justice, when our soldiers and American soldiers come back, can you shout out loudly. We will go to the streets to welcome them for marching into the city taking over Tianjin."

That Thanksgiving Sunday after our house church worship time, Bishop Doctor Liu Yungfang baptized me. Through my earnest begging many times, I was finally allowed to be baptized. I remember I was so sincere, solemn and serious when I knelt down and accepted the Bishop's sprinkling water on my head. I felt the water was from my daddy Jesus. He officially accepted me to be His daughter, so my last name should be "Christ." It was November, the 1944 Thanksgiving season. My baptismal testimony was "the voice from the clouds." From that day I belong to Jesus officially; Jesus Christ is my heavenly Father. As my closing prayer I sang, "Jesus loves me."

Chapter III

A Christmas Remembrance Under Japanese Aggression

After I was baptized, the following Christmas all our family and church family were so happy to celebrate. We knew His birth is the only reason to celebrate, so we never had Santa Claus. I drew a beautiful baby Jesus with hay in the manger, angels, Joseph and Mary, the big star, shepherds and lambs. It was quite a big birthday card. My younger sisters, Margaret and Betty, were then five and four years old. They did their best to draw three wise men and a big camel. We had a hard time recognizing what it was a picture of, but what they made was very colorful with a lot of fingerprints. We put all the cards on the table, next to mom's homemade birthday cake. It was in the shape of a large peach with dozens of little peaches inside, all made with flour, sugar, and oil, steamed, which put color on the peach. In the Chinese tradition, peach means longevity, so whosever birthday it is, that person will receive peaches as gifts. What a beautiful Chinese birthday cake it was! We lighted the candles around the table, gave thanks to the Lord for His coming from heaven to earth to show His humility. From His birth to His death, He came to be our Redeemer, saving us from sin.

My father was an elder of our church and he preached God's word from Philippians 2:15-16. We were touched and uplifted. After prayers only one man and one woman were allowed to sing the hymns with the congregation, humming to prevent the sound of the voices from leaking into the street. Then, after the benediction my father lifted up the big peach cake, blessed and broke it. The little peaches were given to the deacons first, and then the deacons gave the little peaches to everyone. Before we enjoyed it, together we said, "Holy Birthday to Lord Jesus." My father's closing prayer, which I remembered clearly, was, "Father, when You were in the world you had fed more than 5,000 people with two little fish and five loaves. Today we are very few but you can make more people come. Please give us strong faith to trust in You. The harvest time will come. Please help us to stand firmly no matter how bad our situation is. You will be the commander of your Chinese children to spread your gospel to every corner of China. You gave the name of our nation 'Land of God' (Shen-Chou) in our ancient time. Father help us to know how the Chinese used to fear God, worshipping the only one God without image for thousands of years. If we keep the good foundation, then we will be blessed. Father, you can wipe out the Japanese invaders. The Land of God belongs to you. In Jesus' Holy name we pray, Amen."

After this Christmas, Daddy Jesus kept giving us more people to join our church. Many of them were baptized and not only in our church. Other house churches in rural and frontier areas were growing just as fast as we had pleaded for and hoped. My father also shared with our brothers and sisters what his vision was. Now is the time to take the baton from western missionaries with the Lord as our provider. He will help our Chinese indigenous missionaries, you and me to be self-supporting, self-operating to form indigenous ministries in China.

This was the first unforgettable Christmas in my life.

Chapter IV

God Gave the Vision of Indigenous Missions

From 1943 to 1949, my father, David Chang and Bishop C.C. Jiang planted a foundation. The title was "Chinese Christian Self-Supporting, Self-Operating and Self-Evangelizing Million Pounds Foundation" in 1943, and then my father established "New Life Evening Post" Christian Newspaper in 1945. This second wave of Chinese indigenous mission movements led by the believers from western missionaries planted churches. Revival Chinese Christian conferences, grand evangelistic meetings, parades, youth for Christ movements, North West evangelical teams all expanded rapidly. We should praise the Lord for the real religious freedom that the ROC (Republic of China) government gave to us after 1945. At that time, Tianjin Chinese Methodic Wesleyan Church was the office of the "Three Selves Million Pounds Foundation" planted by my father, David Chang and Bishop John C. C. Jiang. After this the Chinese protestant believers increased to over one million. The first wave of Chinese indigenous ministries was led by John Song, Ming-Dao Wang and Watchman Nee in the 1930s.

During the final stage of World War II in 1945, the Allies made three important counter attacks. Together with the U.K, and the Republic of China, the U.S called for the surrender of Japan in the Potsdam Declaration on July 26, 1945, threatening Japan with "prompt and utter destruction" which the Japanese government ignored. The first atomic bomb was dropped on the city of Hiroshima on August 6, 1945, followed by the second one over Nagasaki on

August ninth.

August 15, 1945, six days after the bombings, Japan announced its unconditional surrender to the Allies. The Japanese signed the Instruments of Surrender on September 2, which officially ended World War II. These two bombs are the only nuclear weapons used in war to date. It must be remembered that these bombs are what stopped the killing of innocent people. Fourteen million in China alone were massacred before the war was ended.

The war in Europe ended when Nazi Germany signed its Instrument of Surrender on May 8, 1945. American General Dwight Eisenhower, the supreme commander, led the United States, United Kingdom, and French military forces on D-Day at the Normandy landing to open a second front against Hitler's Nazi armies. Allies attested to the success of D-Day from June 1944. The long-awaited victory happened when the German Nazis finally surrendered on May 8, 1945.

Our family and the Chinese consciously always respect three western heroes and our own Chinese heroes. As a child of China, I knew to honor these leaders:

• Former Prime Minister, Sir Winston Leonard Spencer-Churchill, the greatest wartime leader of the United Kingdom of Britain, particularly during the difficult early days of war, when Britain stood alone in its active opposition to Hitler's Nazi Germany.

• American General Dwight Eisenhower, who led the Allies in the opening of the second front, and the D-Day Normandy landing, which finished World War II.

• United States General McArthur, who led the war in the Pacific realm against brutal Japanese invaders until August 15, 1945 when the Japanese announced its unconditional surrender to the Allies officially ending World War II. General McArthur was the accepter as he signed the Instrument of Unconditional Surrender of Japan on behalf of the Allies.

• Madame Soong May-Ling, First Lady of Former President

Chiang Kai-shik of the Republic of China. She was a Christian. She had tried her best to win lost souls for Christ, among high ranking officers in the government and the military. By God's grace, there were many officers converted to Christ. She joined the social works of women, orphans, education, and charity, among others. She led the home base supplies work for the battlefield. Madam Soong May-Ling was also involved in the national salvation movement, raising funds, and conveying greetings to the wounded soldiers, in the eight years of the Resisting Japanese Invasion War. She also attended many important international meetings in which she played very significant roles. On February 18, 1943, she became the first Chinese national and second woman to address both houses of the U.S. Congress. The response was fervent and supportive. From then on the American military fully supported the Republic of China against Japanese invasion. I respect her very much.

• Famously nicknamed the Flying Tigers, the 1st American Volunteer Group (AVG) of the Chinese Air Force in 1941–1942, was composed of pilots from the United States Army, Navy, and Marine Corps as well as some civilians. These brave pilots were recruited under presidential authority and commanded by Major General Claire Lee Chennault. Interestingly, Soong May-Ling was designated this group's "honorary commander" as she was the bi-lingual person through whom her husband, Generalissimo Chiang Kai-shek and Major General Chennault communicated. The Flying Tigers helped to protect China as they flew dangerous missions and achieved results which gave hope to many that the Japanese could be defeated. The Flying Tiger planes were painted with a highly noticeable shark face, formidable-looking and fierce!

The excellent alarm systems, using radios and telephones in hundreds of small villages stretching far and wide were able to alert the AVG to incoming Japanese fighter planes. Chennault's "dive and zoom" tactics along with the early warning system allowed his pilots to climb to higher altitudes necessary to execute the innovative maneuvers against the more nimble Japanese planes.

In the village of Zhijiang Hunan Province, China is a museum dedicated solely to the Flying Tigers. Their memory is indelibly etched in the black marble wall where all of the names of the AVG pilots and other pilots who died in China are remembered for their sacrifice.

Chapter V

A Special Christmas After the Victory

Christmas in 1945, when our church had a grand celebration, was the most memorable in my life. We cheerfully decorated our sanctuary with Chinese roses, beautiful lanterns, balloons and two-foot tall candles, signifying longevity. Despite the extreme poverty of the church due to the war, we wanted to give gifts to the poor. Two weeks before Christmas, my parents contacted the United States Relief Head Office and the American marine station administrative department to help us give Christmas gifts to thousands of poor children in Tianjin. I loved to help the church family busily, diligently prepare the boxes of candies, warm socks, hats, cookies, and shoes, along with gospel leaflets. Thousands of big boxes were piled up in our church Sunday school area. We organized very well. Our plan was that the kids be divided into ten lines, each line having three people serve the kids. At the end of every line would be American marines carrying a big basket full of gift boxes.

As it began snowing on that Christmas Eve, our church was broadcasting Christmas carols with loud speakers facing the streets. The people walked past the church and were enjoying the scene with brilliant lights in the night. Their hearts were made lighter and brighter. Beautiful sounds of carols attracted the attention of people to come to church to listen to the Messiah and the pastor's preaching after the service. I remember running around every line and helping the sisters and brothers to distribute the gift boxes. The kids, surprised and cheerfully holding the boxes, left from another door to show the box to their parents. Waiting outside kids were lined up to continue to receive the gifts. When the marines' baskets were empty, another usher would put more gift boxes in. Even though there were thousands of poor kids, the organization done so far in advance helped to make the distribution of the Christmas gift program a success.

I was sweating, singing, running around the kids and I thought that there will be no "poor little match girl" dying that night. I remember seeing the marines also sweating and smiling, but continuing to greet every kid, "Merry Christmas" and the kids shouted "Dinghao," a thumbs up sign, signaling to them, "You are the best!" Outside, the world was all covered by white snow like the drawing on Christmas cards. Daddy Jesus' blood can make me white as snow. But the love of Christ has given the poor children a warm well-fed Christmas through us and American marines.

On Christmas day we had a wonderful Messiah concert along with a worship service. The musician team included an orchestra and famous vocal soloists. I was eager to join the eighty-member choir. Unfortunately, I was too young. I could not help myself, however, when the choir sang the Hallelujah chorus. From the congregation seat I stood up with everybody to sing, "King of Kings, and Lord of Lords," adding to the great praising sound which surely reached the throne of heaven. What a lovely, wonderful, glorious Christmas in my life.

Chapter VI

Memories of Survivors

In August 1945, the Japanese pleaded an unconditional surrender to the Allied Forces: The United States, China, Russia, France, and the United Kingdom. General MacArthur was the chief representative of the U.S. at that time. I believe the big victory belongs to the justice the Lord provided.

As I am writing, thinking of those long ago good days of the Chinese people celebrating the victory of resisting aggressive war, I am still excited. It was unforgettable. The music of the radio broadcasts, instead of groaning, moaning Japanese opera, perhaps only for me then, gave forth with beautiful classical symphonies. There were Chinese children's songs, and even Christian hymns. The one I cherish the most was "The Stars and Stripes Forever." Whenever that was played, the volume was raised by every resident who had a radio.

I remember we eagerly climbed to the roof of our three-story house to watch the many airplanes flying by. Hailing the airplanes, we called out, "You are the best"... (Dinghao) "Welcome, you heroes." Sometimes the airplanes flew so low we could see the pilots' smiling faces and the hands waving to all of our cheering people, as the planes distributed leaflets. People were standing everywhere, on the streets, roofs and even on the trees and the posts. They were waving the Chinese national flags with the white sun and the blue and red background, as well as American flags.

While people were shouting, jumping up and down, smiling,

waving flags, and congratulating each other, many of them were crying. Shedding tears like springs bursting forth, they were missing their lost ones, those husbands, children, parents...the beloved ones who sacrificed their lives on battlefields, in prisons, or were killed in Japanese bombardments. I am thinking of the pilots of the famous "Flying Tigers" air force troops, both American and Chinese pilots in combat union. Although they had all victories in every air combat mission, they suffered heavy casualties. Most of the remains of those heroes could never be found.

I believe that whenever the enemies surrender we should forgive them. Nevertheless, for the martyrs' sake and for the truth of history, we have to remember the serious crimes that Nazi Germany and the Japanese militarists committed. Survivors cannot forget who rescued them, nor who paid the tragic price fighting against the inhumane invaders for the peace and freedom of the world.

We cannot distort history and cannot be devoid of gratitude to the rescuers. That was the glorious, victorious history of the United States of America, the Republic of China and the Allied Forces.

I remember our Chinese kids and the Chinese people giving a thumbs up to the American soldiers when they were stationed in Tianjin. They met in the streets and said to them "Dinghao" which means "You are the best." I especially loved to watch the military band when they practiced the marching songs and other beautiful songs. I was thrilled to see the conductor waving his baton. I learned their songs and the music right away. One of my favorites is, "Oh yes, home again, and home again America for me." I also loved their chocolates and the Coca Cola Marines loved to give to kids.

Chapter VII

An Unexpected Christmas Celebration in 1953

Beginning in 1949, the Chinese communists came to power, after we had experienced four years of complete religious freedom. After the Korean War Premier Chou-En-Lai used unbeliever Wu-Yao-Zong to establish "TSPM" - Three Selves Patriotic Movement. They stole the original title of Three Selves, founded by my father, David Chang, and changed to Self-supporting, Self-operating, and Self-evangelizing Patriotic Movement Association. The theme of the original Three Selves Foundation was to love the Lord, be faithful to the Lord, and to evangelize China. Their theme of the new Three Selves Patriotic Movement Association is "love the communist country, love the government, and love the church".

During the eight years Japanese occupation from 1937-1945, my dad was under house arrest by the Japanese. My mother sold the jewelry from her dowry to support our family of eleven members. She also financially supported my dad as he started the original Three Selves Foundation and the New Life Evening Post newspaper. Because of this, our family had very little income to live on.

A townsman, Mr. Shiao-Shian Wang, CEO and president of Shanghai Salt Industrial Bank, found out about our difficulties and gave my mother 800 silver dollar coins to buy Christmas gifts for us children. But my father had another plan to celebrate Christmas in a Chinese way for our church. He decided to decorate with Chinese lanterns, tall candles, flowers, balloons, and long red silk sheets with golden scriptures hanging around the church posts. Those decorations surely cost a lot of money. My dad asked my mom, "Shall we buy gifts for our kids or buy gifts for Jesus?" Without hesitation my mom gave all the 800 silver dollar coins to my dad for that purpose. We children felt so sad for our Christmas gifts that we had dreamed of for so long, it vanished like bubbles. My mom explained, "The Lord will give us more."

Two days before Christmas Eve, all the new decorations were done. Our sanctuary looked fantastic. Sadly, that day Mr. Xiao-Peng-Yang, an unbeliever and the chairman of TSPM in Tianjin, removed what the church families had created. He pulled down all the decorations from the sanctuary and returned all of the flowers, candles, and the long red silk sheets to our home. As my father was the chief elder of our church, Mr. Yang showed some respect. However, when we asked why, he replied, "As long as there is a virtuous and gentle wife at home, the husband would not do evil deeds." This event broke our family's heart. My parents were silent and stopped my shouting, "This is not right!" as Mr. Yang left.

My parents and my older brothers separately sent flowers, lanterns, and candles to believers' homes. The long red silk sheets were quickly mailed to our sister church, Beijing Methodist. My parents wanted us to have a real silent and holy night to remember our Christ's birthday at home with no decorations, only the star and manger. That Christmas Eve and Christmas Day many church members, almost 90 percent, did not attend church. From then on only a few women came to church.

When the volunteers who made them learned that Mr. Yang pulled down all the new Chinese decorations for Christmas, they preferred to celebrate at home secretly. The flowers and lanterns which we sent to them made their Christmas more delightful.

With the advent of the church being controlled by TSPM, the pastors' sermons were twisting the Bible truth, watered down God's word and quoted out of Bible context. Believers could not agree with TSPM. They knew only Christ Jesus is the master of His church and not the communist government.

Our family had a very special Christmas Eve service. I helped my mother make a one stair stage in the sitting room. We hung a blue curtain and a very bright six angled star as background. I then put my doll to be the baby Jesus, in a make-shift manger, really just a wooden box. There were no Christmas decorations or manger scenes available to buy in any shops. The baby Jesus was all alone.

All the lights were turned off except for the star shining on Jesus and the lamp for the piano. My younger brother Joe played carols as my father read Scripture telling of the birth of Christ. Then my father prayed. We sang all the Christmas carols, even several parts of "The Messiah." My mother sang beautifully as first soprano while my other brother, Caleb, sang the bass part. Some former choir members came to join our family celebration. We had no cake nor goodies, as my mom was in no mood to make the traditional peach cake. We kept singing until late. We loved to be companions for our lonely baby Jesus.

I kept the manger and baby Jesus for a long time. This unforgettable Christmas made me think of the Scriptures which my father read *"...Though the world was made through Him, the world did not recognize Him. He came to that which was His own, but His own did not receive Him...to those who believed in His name, He gave the right to become God's children"* (John 1:10-12). Oh, daddy Jesus I am your child, I was your companion when you were a little lonely baby. I am God's child, that's for sure! My father changed my Christian name from Mary to Dorothy after Christmas. I asked him the reason. He said, "You will know when you grow up." This was the most unexpected Christmas in my life. I learned that the real meaning of Christmas is not in decorations, but intimacy with Him.

Chapter VIII

Christmas in a Communist Hard Labor Camp

In 1960 when I was put into a hard labor camp for my faith I experienced the bitter cold in winter. Everyone felt as if they were freezing to death. A lot of prisoners suffered frostbite. Because of this, made worse by having no heat, the guards were afraid of losing prisoners to work for them. They allowed every one of us to have an empty IV bottle that we filled with hot water to warm up our quilts.

On Christmas Eve my bottle broke, saturating my bedclothes such that my freezing body prevented sleep. I had to wear all my clothes and sit against the wall beside my mattress made of hay. I felt like the "poor little match girl" in Hans Christian Andersen's tale. Hugging my shivering body, I prayed with tears, "Lord, would you please hug me? I am freezing to death." The next day I reported to the guard and he allowed me to have another bottle from the first aid station. My quilt was still wet and useless to warm my chilled body. I again sat against the wall and put my bottle with hot water into my clothes. Holding it tightly, I prayed again.

A miracle happened! My bottle was still warm when I woke up the next morning when the whistles sounded for us to get up and go to the labor field. That bottle kept me warm the whole night. This poor lonely girl of God did not freeze to death but instead slept well. I did not tell anyone else what happened. I kept the bottle for six years. That was my Lord hugging me every night. How could I not give thanks with a grateful heart to my Savior? I remember when I was little I used to call Him daddy Jesus. When I was put into jail for

Him I started to call Him my Savior, my Lord. My Savior hugged me that night and into Christmas morn. What an unforgettable Christmas full of mercy and grace!

Chapter IX

Freedom at Last—My First Christmas in America

In 1980, after surviving captivity for 20 years I was freed by the government. They restored my reputation, announcing my case and treatment were wrong. Yet I praise the Lord for His grace and mercy by choosing to mold, shape and rebuild me. Although I received no settlement in worldly terms for those lost 20 years, the Lord got my heart totally. The political situation still resisted Christians giving testimony and spreading the gospel to people outside the government-controlled TSPM church. Yet His calling to and in my heart was clear --"To be my witness." I responded, "Yes, my Lord. I will be your witness."

My Lord worked on my situation in wonderful and unbelievable ways. I came to the United States of America as a visiting medical scholar at UNC Chapel Hill. That first Christmas season in 1984 I got a chance to listen to a Messiah rehearsal. I was sitting in the last pew in a big church. I was enjoying every sound of the Messiah with tears, because I could not sing anymore. My God-given voice was taken away after 20 years, tracing back to torture suffered in prison. After my release from jail I went to see the doctor. After checking me thoroughly, the doctor told me my vocal cords had nodes. He said to me, "Give up your dream of singing. Try some Chinese herbs. Maybe you can at least talk well."

But the herbs did not work on me. As the fans of holy music all stood up to sing along with the choir on the Hallelujah chorus, I could not stop myself. I thought no matter how bad my voice, I yearned to sing along with them. As I sang a couple of verses, I felt something in my throat. It hurt very much. I had to swallow and then I found out my voice became clearer. I could not believe it. I placed my two hands around my ears so that I could hear more clearly. That normal voice was coming from me! I continued to sing and the voice got better and better. My heart was trembling with shock! Through tears of joy I gave thanks to my Lord - "You are my King of Kings, Lord of Lords." From then on I continued to sing along with the choir.

God led my best friend Miss Mary Frances Boyce, a great violinist, to introduce me to a famous Christian soprano vocalist. The idea was to have Mrs. Peacock coach me. She suggested I sing the solo part, "I Know My Redeemer Liveth," at the Messiah concert. While I had a good voice when I was young, my reborn voice did not qualify me to sing this solo part, I thought. Mrs. Peacock, having other ideas, said, "Your spiritual walk makes you suitable to sing this part." Under her teaching and practicing two to three times, I stood on the stage the night of the Christmas Messiah Sing Along concert. My heart was so excited and I said to my Lord, "Today I will be your witness telling people you are wonderful, Almighty God. You healed my 20-year-long hoarse voice. Now, my reborn voice only sings songs of praise to you."

While I do not know how the people responded, I did my best. The only One I wanted to please was my Lord. That was the fifth unforgettable Christmas in my life. I continue singing for Him alone.

Chapter X

The Lord Uses Two Men

After my reputation was restored and the wrong case finished, the government told me, "Now you are free. You are supposed to go back to Beijing Medical University, but you are already over 40 years old and cannot be a student. We will forward your file to the Ministry of Public Health. They will allocate you a proper job in a hospital or somewhere else. You just keep waiting. But there is a rule for you and all the other people who were wrongly treated and already had their verdicts reversed. You cannot tell any foreigners about your case, so please remember that."

I moved to Beijing. Carrying my twin sons Joseph and Daniel to meet my husband, Freddie Sun, gave us the happiest family reunion. But I kept waiting for two months and there was no news from the Ministry of Public Health. I used to pray to my Lord, "Dear Lord, you know I have been in forced hard labor camp and in the jail for 20 long years. I forgot all my knowledge in the medical field. Please give me only a humble job as housekeeper, babysitter or cook. That's good enough for me. I just want to support my family."

One day my dear close friend Miss Daisy Lee, sympathetic and loving me very much, invited me to her place. As we had been school mates, she wanted me to help with her English skills. She already practiced her medical skills as a physician for 20 years. But after the American President Nixon visited China, the government allowed the school and intellectuals to learn English. If you wanted to raise your position, you had to pass the English test. She knew I was the better one in English compared to others, so I went to help.

Just a short time after I arrived at Daisy's place, a middle-aged gentleman knocked on the door. Daisy was not in a pleasant mood to introduce this man to me, so just said, "He is a high-ranking officer in the Ministry of Public Health." We greeted each other and he asked me, "Which hospital are you working with?" I answered, "I have no job." He was so surprised because Daisy just introduced me to him as her college friend. He continued to ask me many questions. Daisy was so mad she said, "Dorothy suffered badly for 20 years for an unjust sentence. She was in labor camps and jail for that long only because you Communists have a bad policy, treating innocent young Christians as counter-revolutionaries. Now, she is waiting for a job even though the government already corrected this wrong case totally."

The man replied right away, "Maybe I can help" but I refused him saying, "I am not qualified to be a medical doctor and I cannot be a nurse either because I did not study to be a nurse." That man explained why he so much wanted to offer help. "There was a job open to be a medical editor working for the United Nations World Health Organization. But only an insider in MPH could apply for it." He said, "I could apply for this chance for you but you must pass two tests of medical knowledge, and the translation skills." I said, "Please do not, because I could not pass the tests..." Before I could finish my words, Daisy shouted at him, "Are you sure? Please do that; it will be no harm at all if Dorothy fails the test." The man smiled and nodded, looking so proud of himself. Offering this help to me made Daisy very pleased. Later I discovered this fellow kept visiting Daisy trying to persuade her to marry him. He was definitely not Daisy's type.

I prayed again, "My Lord, my master, what are You doing? You know I am not qualified to take these tests. I could not handle a job as an editor. I have almost forgotten all the medical terms. I just asked you for a job as a babysitter or housekeeper. What do You want me to do?" That night the Lord gave me only one sentence: "Do not be afraid, only trust in Me."

One week later, I went to the place where the tests were held. I was scared to death as I knew that everyone else in the room was a medical doctor. Everyone had two books on the table, so I got two books as well. The man who was in charge announced, "You have 90 minutes to do the translation, English to Chinese and Chinese to English." My two books were "The Forum of World Health" and "The Pestology." When I saw the others working so fast on the paper I felt dizzy. I translated only three to four pages of English to Chinese, spending more time on Chinese to English. When the time was up, I was the last one to hand over my paper. I figured I might get a D minus. On the way back home I cried. I was very upset feeling both hopeless and full of shame. But my Lord kept telling me, "Do not be afraid, just trust in Me."

The next day I went into the other room for the oral English test. They tested us individually. People one by one went in and left, until they asked me, "Are you ready?"… When I got into the room, I recognized a chief thoracic surgeon among several old professors seated behind the long table. At the left end of the table there was a very obese high-ranking officer. At the right end of the table was a foreign blue-eyed gentleman. Those professors started to question me in English. Thank God, I understood what they were saying. Immediately I answered in English just a couple of questions. The foreigner said, "Please, may I ask her a question?" That grossly overweight officer immediately answered him with a big smile. "Of course, you may, please go ahead." The foreigner asked me, "When and where did you learn your English? You have a strong American accent." I hesitated and looked at that rotund officer. He right away encouraged me, "Tell him the truth! Don't worry."

I thought "Oh, Lord, are you working in his heart?" I said, "I was educated by American missionaries. They taught me English since I was three years old from church kindergarten through Sunday school and in a private Christian girls' school." ....Oh boy, what would this Communist officer think? With a look of interest the foreigner asked those professors, "May I see her resume?" The professors looked at that officer waiting for his permission. He said, "Of course," with a smile, so the foreigner got it. My resume gave him a big surprise for it was only one page. Graduate of an American Christian private school and girls' high school, Beijing Medical University, not finished, and then there was only blank paper. He asked me with a suspicious look, "Where have you been? Why did you drop your studies?" Oh boy! "Sir, I really cannot answer this question."

Now everybody looked at the officer. To my great surprise, as I had already shaken my head to the foreigner, the officer still maintained, "You can tell him why, only the truth." His expression, however, belied his response. What a special spectacle, my heart kept praying, "My Savior, my Master, if I tell them all the truth that will be completely breaking the rules which the public security officers told me. Please give me the proper words."

I saw all the waiting eyes. Then I told everybody very briefly that my wrong case has lasted 20 years from July 1960 to July 1980. I didn't tell them about all of the tortures, backbreaking labor, insults and the brainwashing, starvation, danger, and violence. I only told them I was a Christian and refused to deny my faith. I went on to explain, although I have forgotten the knowledge of the medical field, I have skillful hands for working on a rice farm, at a factory as a miller, turner, bench worker… and I worked at the jail hospital as a doctor's assistant for several years during the labor time. If you have a job open in a hospital as a nurse assistant, I would love to try.

When I stopped my answer, all the people in that room looked at each other silently. With a serious expression the foreigner silently looked at my resume once more and gave it back to the professors. Finally, they told me, "Okay, you may go now, we will give you notice of the result of your tests."

Confused, I left that building with fear, shame and disgrace. My

Lord, what is your purpose? What do You want me to do? You know that I must fail the test, so why do you open only this door for me? It was not only my own failure, but also I made You lose face....The only thing I can do is cry with disgrace. My Lord, you even led me to a very dangerous situation that tomorrow may bring the security officers to arrest me.....You have told me, "Don't be afraid, only trust in Me."

About two weeks later a big envelope reached me from the Ministry of Public Health. With two trembling hands I opened it. It was a notice so startling that I couldn't believe it. I was engaged as a medical editor on three months of probative time, depending upon my working achievement, to be employed permanently or not, they will let me know.

Chapter XI

How I Came to America

In the three months of probation, I made a great effort to learn editing and do a good job. My Lord helped me to learn the editing. At the same time he opened another door for me to be the interpreter working for the WHO offices and MPH offices. When they visited China for meetings, conferences, observation, and negotiations, they always had luxurious banquets, went sightseeing and shopping. They inevitably needed me as their interpreter. After 20 years of being a prisoner and night parolee, my Lord led me to "The Chinese Great Hall of the People," luxurious restaurants, five-star hotels and comfortable great sightseeing tours as part of my new job.

Three months later, I was formally hired as an editor. My efforts were recognized leading to my position as the responsible editor on two forum magazines of WHO one year later. The rank of this position is equal to a university lecturer. My Lord was continually working on something bigger. For His purpose was molding and making me to be His witness.

In 1984 I got a chance to go to the U.S. as a medical visiting scholar at UNC at Chapel Hill, N.C. I chose public health class as an advanced study, for my former major was dentistry. I was now working in this field of public health. My boss asked me to build a bridge for Chinese medical experts and American experts to exchange visits for special projects. In July 1984, I came to America for the first time. Now I have a deeper understanding of King David's words in Psalm 103: 1-2, 6, 8-13

Psalm 103:1-2, 6

"Praise the Lord, my soul; all my inmost being, praise his holy name. Praise the Lord, my soul, and forget not all his benefits—; . . . The Lord works righteousness and justice for all the oppressed."

Psalm 103:8-13

"The Lord is compassionate and gracious, slow to anger, abounding in love. He will not always accuse, nor will he harbor his anger forever; he does not treat us as our sins deserve or repay us according to our iniquities. For as high as the heavens are above the earth, so great is his love for those who fear him; as far as the east is from the west, so far has he removed our transgressions from us. As a father has compassion on his children, so the Lord has compassion on those who fear him;"

And His words in II Samuel 7: 20-22

"What more can David say to you? For you know your servant, Sovereign Lord. For the sake of your word and according to your will, you have done this great thing and made it known to your servant. How great you are, Sovereign Lord! There is no one like you, and there is no God but you, as we have heard with our own ears."

Chapter XII

Robert Hodgson's Story in China

By Robert A. Hodgson, Ph.D — China 1945

I had arrived in Tientsin with my radio unit via the Hai River from Taku a scant two weeks before, although the first Marine Division, of which my unit was a part, had been sent to North China to implement the surrender of the Japanese armed forces there and to oversee the repatriation of Japanese soldiers and civilians to Japan. When we entered Tientsin we had been most warmly welcomed by the citizens of the city. For them the long and repressive occupation by the Japanese was finally over and a new future beckoned. The central part of the city was European in nature, with the buildings reflecting the nationality, and it was the first civilization we had seen since leaving San Diego; and we were most anxious to get liberty to explore the shops and other entertainment.

On the first Sunday, as we strolled down one of the main streets looking into stores, we spied a large sign ahead on our side of the street. It was in what appeared to be English. We saw it read "Wesleyan Methodist Church." This was the same denomination of Protestant church I had been attending at home in Baltimore. I was astonished and my two buddies much intrigued. The church itself looked very much as if it had been transplanted, as is, from some town in the United States. The doors of the church were open and there was a sound of joyous singing. I recognized a tune, but not the words. We climbed the steps and carefully peeked in the front door.

By this time members of the congregation had turned to see the cause of the interruption. They began to smile and one, probably the Deacon, came to the door, and we found ourselves being escorted down the center aisle to the very first row of pews. The service was resumed – in Chinese. It was obviously a service of thanksgiving for the liberation of the city and the prospect for a brighter future.

At the end of the service the congregation crowded around and personally welcomed us to their fellowship. A number of the older people as well as several young people about our age spoke enough English. It was at this time that a charming lady about my own mother's age introduced herself as Mrs. Miriam Chang. She spoke good English and, during our conversation, she learned I frequently attended a Wesleyan Methodist church at my home in Baltimore. It was then Mrs. Chang offered me the most generous invitation to visit her house at evening mealtime. She then gave me directions to her house in the former British sector of Tientsin. And so it was that I found myself standing on an October evening in front of the House of Chang.

It was a pleasant, early evening in October, 1945. I found myself, a young United States Marine Corporal, standing in front of a large, three story Victorian style brick house in the former British concession of Tientsin. I was responding to a very gracious invitation by Mrs. Chang to have an evening meal at her home any time I was off duty and free to do so. This was an unexpected opportunity for me to learn a little about Chinese family life and I wondered what the evening might have in store. I reflected for a moment on the unlikely circumstances that had brought about the invitation.

I climbed the front steps and spied a bell button next to the massive oak front door. I pressed the button and heard a bell ring faintly. A man opened the door and motioned me to enter into a large front hall where I was asked to wait. I stood, somewhat nervously, looking at the furniture and decorative pieces in the hall. The door at the end of the hall opened and Mrs. Chang appeared. She greeted me cordially and told me to follow her back through the door into a large dining room. A long table was set in the middle of the room. At one end were several young men of roughly my own age and at the other a number of young girls. They were waiting for me. Mrs. Chang introduced me around and I was greeted cordially by the young men and the girls. Mrs. Chang explained to them that I wished to learn something of Chinese ways and home life, Chinese table manners and the proper use of chopsticks. This was greeted with great good humor by the youngsters who appeared more than ready to take my education in hand.

I was soon seated between two of the girls. As a beginner this was most appropriate. On my left was a young lady of about eight or nine years. Obviously a person of character, she immediately took charge correcting my first attempts to use the chopsticks. The young lady's name was Mary Chang, who the readers will recognize as the Christian missionary and author Dorothy Sun and that is how I first met her! When I could make a late afternoon or evening visit to the Changs' house, if I arrived early, I might be drawn into playing some Chinese children's game with Mary and her young sisters. At meals my education in Chinese table protocol proceeded apace under Mary's strict supervision. Meals always were accompanied with much good natured banter and laughter. The food was always delicious. In this atmosphere of good fellowship I came to know the generous and loving Chang family. Initially, I saw Mr. Chang only briefly as he was constantly going to business meetings. I was touched by his kindness toward me.

By November, I had become proficient with chopsticks and had acquired formal Chinese table manners. In conversations with Mrs. Chang I soon learned of her involvement with the YWCA of which she was the head in Tientsin. My mother's sister had made a career in the YWCA and my father and his father were career YMCA men. And so, many bonds of common interest were established. One evening, I was greeted by Mr. Chang and informed I was to have dinner with him and his guests. He smiled and I realized I had successfully completed my course in Chinese table manners. I was quickly put at ease by Mr. Chang as he introduced me to them. We all entered the formal dining room. The conversation was mostly in English and I realized Mr. Chang was highly regarded by his guests. Guests included correspondents, political leaders, and high ranking military men. It was clear that Mr. Chang, or "H.C.," was a very influential leader in planning for China's future. He was always on the go, running the newspaper he had established, "The New Life Evening Post," and generally working for the welfare of the Tientsin Community. He was a Christian in the best sense and set an example of Christian living and giving.

Mary, now known as Dorothy, I realized took very much after her father in temperament and organizational ability. She and I became, in Marine parlance "great buddies." I became accepted almost as a member of the family. H.C. and Mrs. Chang were almost the identical ages of my parents. They made me feel thoroughly at home in a strange land through their Christian love and generosity to a young U.S. Marine Corporal who had not seen his home in more than two years. Through the Changs, I also made friends with a number of Chinese young men and women of my own age. The Wesleyan Methodist Church was planning a great Christmas celebration including singing Handel's Messiah. I had joined the church choir to participate, along with other Marines. Life in Tientsin had become unexpectedly pleasant.

One year later, my unit received orders to move north. Mrs. Chang was visibly upset when I gave her the news. She had counted on me to celebrate Christmas with her family. Mary cried and said a tearful farewell to her Marine buddy whom she had come to regard as an older brother. The older boys quickly organized a formal farewell dinner for me at a fine restaurant the next evening. We spent an enjoyable evening at the end of which we had a formal picture taken. A couple of days later Mrs. Chang, who knew the North

China winter was harsh, promised me an old Chinese riding coat lined with fur she had to keep me warm, but I had to leave before she could give it to me. This led later to a rather amazing incident. We were billeted at Pei Tai Ho beach. The second day the Captain called me into his office. I wondered what it might portend. The Captain had a large brown paper wrapped package under his arm. It was addressed to me and had been delivered the several miles from Pei Tai Ho by a Chinese Nationalist soldier. The Captain was more than a little curious, as well he might be. I opened the package immediately and found a fur-lined Chinese riding jacket along with a note from Mrs. Chang saying that as General Yen was going to Pei Tai Ho she had asked him to drop off the package for me. In this he most courteously obliged, stopping his troop train long enough to have the package delivered. This was so typically thoughtful of Mrs. Chang and very kind of General Yen.

The winter had turned very cold and the fur-lined jacket kept me warm even on the coldest days. I have kept the coat for all those years as a reminder of the love and kindness of Mrs. Chang and of the whole family that gave a "home" to a young U.S. Marine so long away from his own family in America. I spent that Christmas in An Shan with many thoughts of two families, one in Tientsin and one in Baltimore. In January, we were hustled onto a troop train to Tientsin, where we spent overnight in a large warehouse. No one was allowed to leave or communicate with friends in the city. There was no chance for farewells and I left China with sadness at leaving my "family" and joy at the prospect of going home. For awhile I kept in touch with my Chinese friends and the Chang family by mail. One day I received a letter saying that the Communist forces were on the outskirts of Tientsin and the future was uncertain. He asked that I not write again until I heard from him.

I wondered how H.C. and Mrs. Chang were faring under the new regime, the fate of the Wesleyan Methodist Church, the YWCA and that of Christians in general. I wondered how Mary would grow up in a Communist world. In *Clay in the Potter's Hand* Dorothy and her husband, Freddie Sun, have answered those questions in their graphic accounts of their years of struggle to keep their faith and survive the many attempts by the Communists to crush their spirits.

Thirty-eight years had passed when in March of 1984 I received a letter from Dorothy written in 1982. It had finally found me through the editor of the International Association of Retired YMCA Directors. In August, Dorothy was able to visit my wife Lorna and me in Pittsburgh for a joyful reunion. After nearly 40 years, we met again.

In 2011 Lorna and I traveled 100 miles to Charlottesville, Virginia to see Dorothy and visit Christian Aid Mission. We had another very happy reunion. At that meeting I gave back to Dorothy the very same fur-lined coat I had kept for 60 years! We are still in contact with each other.

The rest of the story is Dorothy's. She has suffered much and accomplished more. Her early family life and Christian upbringing provided her the means and the will to overcome her persecutions and, as a Christian missionary today, carry her message back to the remotest regions of China. Enjoy her story.

Robert Hodgson's
Chinese godmother and
a little baby girl

Robert Hodgson in 1945

Left,
Reunion with
Robert in Pittsburg,
PA 1984

Right,
Robert Hodgson
and his wife, Lorna

Chapter XIII

Finding Robert Hodgson

In 1983 before I came to the U.S., my mother was 83 years old. She lost her eyesight from diabetes and after breast cancer surgery, her health slowly declined. But her heart was still full of love, kindness and sweetness. My family had moved to Beijing in 1980 so she missed my twin sons Joseph and Daniel very much. She missed her old friends as well, because most of them left to live in America. My baby sister Grace, whom my mother loved most, had moved to Hong Kong. I tried to locate her old friends, but the addresses were lost when the Red Guards burned our personal records in 1966. My father's books, the 40 photo albums and directories, and letters were totally destroyed from 1966 – 1976 during the great calamitous cultural revolution.

I knew my mother loved her American godson, Robert Hodgson, very much and I also remembered his father was the General Secretary of the YMCA in Maryland. We really missed the good old days when Robert was with our family. He called my mother "Mom," who treated him like a son. I asked God to please help me to find him, which would make my mother very happy. I decided to write a letter to the General Secretary of Maryland YMCA in 1982. I was hoping for information to help me locate Mr. Robert Hodgson, whose father had been in the same position at the YMCA 37 years earlier. Very soon, a letter from Maryland arrived. After the current General Secretary learned our story, he felt God put a burden on his heart. He must help me by paying more attention to anyone who may be related to the Hodgson family.

One year later, a beautiful letter written by Robert Hodgson's mother arrived from the U.S. It was a big surprise for her to receive a letter from the YMCA which mentioned the Chang family eager to find the Hodgson family. She wrote that several weeks before, she had submitted an article to the magazine of the YMCA. The editor found out the writer's last name was Hodgson. Robert's mother still remembered how her son had a Chinese godmother named Miriam. The Chang family was the only place he loved to go because they loved him so much. Robert told her he had two homes, one in the U.S. and one in Tianjin, China.

Clearly our Lord is omnipresent, penetrating hearts everywhere. Miracles are His specialty. He alone is wonderful! My mother went to Paradise in February 1985. There was no chance to see her beloved godson again until we all will meet in heaven some day.

Robert received a very meaningful Chinese name (Ho Jue Sheng), 賀(Ho) (celebrate) 巨(Jue) (great) 勝(Sheng) (victory). He still can write his Chinese name correctly. I still think of Robert as my dear older brother. I remember many of his fine qualities. He used his talented, skillful hands to help in any way he could. He always asked my mom, "Is there anything such as a radio, clock or telephone that needs to be fixed? Mom, I can do it well." He also loved to learn new things: how to eat noodles or peas with chopsticks. He was pleased to learn Chinese table manners, as well as games we young girls liked to play: hide and seek, Chinese checkers, and three-legs-jump, what you would call a three-legged race. Another skill he mastered was calculation with a Chinese abacus, which really surprised everybody, as it is quite difficult. He was also good at drawing.

Robert was a good, decent boy of 18, ten years older than I at the time he came into our lives. He liked going to church, singing in the choir and coming to our house. There he spent long evenings with us kids, running back to the military station only five minutes before the bedtime bugle blew. He never dealt with any activities in "red light" districts.

His roommates once asked him, "Hey, where do you go every evening? We did not see you at dinner time and the whole night before bed time." Robert told my mom, "Mom, I told them, I go to a nice family's home where every day there is always a lot of fun and delicious dinners. They asked again, 'Fun with whom?' I said, 'Four girls!' They pleaded immediately, 'Take us with you, please.'" Rolling his eyes, Robert answered them with, "No, No!" He always made us laugh. My mom said, "Son, remember, send to your mother the money you put away. She will be so happy and proud of you." Robert was always very gentle to my mother. "I will, Mom."

One day when I got back home from school, I saw my mom talking with Robert in the sitting room. Both of them were in tears. My mom gave him a big warm hug and ordered the cook to add some more of Robert's favorite dishes to the menu. We had a rich farewell dinner and everybody felt sad. I cried and lost my appetite. My older brothers, Joe and Caleb, invited Robert and some of the other choir boys for a farewell dinner in a fancy restaurant the next day. For me, it meant losing my best playmate, best gentle older "brother" and a very nice member of our family.

Chapter XIV

The Best Christian Mother

Whenever I think about my mother, Mrs. Miriam Neh Chang, I give thanks and praise to the Lord for the precious gift of such a mom. She was not only beautiful, but kind, sweet, gifted and full of love like the Proverbs 31 woman. She has been a tremendous influence for good in many respects.

My mother was a professional operatic soprano. When I was in her womb she continued to exercise her singing voice every day. When I was in the cradle she played music all the time. If I became cranky, she would put on special music that calmed me down right away. Mom related how the beautiful lullabies she sang to me lulled me to sleep. Being exposed to such beautiful music even before I was born must have given me the great love for music I have had all of my life.

At five years old I began to take piano lessons. My mom invited a famous Chinese woman pianist to be my abecedarian. Miss Myrtle J.D. Liu was a strict teacher which was good for me. I lost any chance of practicing the piano from 1952 to 1984, but when I came to the U.S. I still remembered how to play. With the use of only nine fingers, having suffered a bone fracture on my right little finger during my imprisonment, I was still able to play for my Chinese church in Charlottesville.

As a young child I always loved to sing. When I reached the age of 12, my mother began to coach me. She taught me how to breathe, as well as how to use the mouth to create sweet and mellow tones.

Singing for the Lord, whether as a soloist, a leading part in the choir, or in a sing-along, provides me with one of the most joyful and exciting things in my life.

Another lesson my mother taught me was how to dress myself properly. She understood the importance of dressing appropriately for both the occasion and the occupation. I learned from her to dress in a dignified fashion, paying attention to color, pattern, my age, stage and position in life. She taught me how to coordinate everything, from the wearing of jewelry - gorgeous not gaudy - to shoes, bag and accessories. My mother could never imagine, however, what kind of clothing her daughter would wear in prison, nor what she herself would be wearing during the ten years of the cultural revolution calamity. I thank both God and my mother for making me never look gaudy.

As the daughter of a rich and successful businessman, as well as being famous in the music field, my mother certainly had many gentlemen admirers. But she chose to marry my father, David H. Chang, a widower with five children and a dilapidated house needing much repair. A well-educated man having studied in Japan, France and the United States, he was also president of the Chinese Painting Company. The key to their marrying was a very deep love and her willingness to become the stepmother of his five children. My mother also had a vision from God that her husband's name must be David. My father loved and served the Lord with all his heart. So she gave all her love to them, and helped to rebuild my father's home.

My mother was happy to help my father financially to start The Three Selves Million Pounds Foundation and help to create the New Life Evening Post. During the eight years of the Japanese occupation my father was under house arrest. As the family had no income during that time, my mom had to support the whole family by selling her jewelry. Her last diamond ring was given to my elder brother's fiancé. My mom gave her daughters-in-law and my elder sister the last of her money. Mrs. David Chang was known for her kindness, generosity, and her complete loving care of her step-children. This generous woman became a wonderful testimony to them and to the community.

Miriam Chang was a good and faithful president of the YWCA of Tianjin from 1923 to 1949. At that time the organization was truly a Young Women's Christian Association where the Lord was honored and respected. My mother gave her time, energy, gifts and sacrificial service to the Lord in this capacity. The YWCA provided many good services to the community, including spreading the gospel to the people. When the Communists took over Tianjin, the Young Women's Christian Association no longer was allowed to have religious activities. My mother was very angry. No more Christian activities, no more Miriam. That is when my mom stepped down. I will always remember her strong stand and faithfulness to the Lord.

Just because of her, our family life was always full of love, laughter, music, parties, and church meetings. Household harmony came from house rules my mother established: there would be no shouting, quarrels, jealousy, prejudice, nor favoritism. Mom also treated the servants like friends. After 1949 we could no longer afford to pay them. They all got good jobs at the Beijing Union Hospital after they left our house, as cook-cleaning lady and service personnel in the Doctor's Compound. My aunt, Miss Vera Neh (PhD), the principal of the Chinese Nursing Education Institute, who was so close to her only sister Miriam, assisted our help in getting these positions.

◆ HE ALONE ◆

Chapter XV

Testimonies of My Father

After I was born on May 29th, 1936 in Tianjin, my father began to work for the government. He had two new jobs. He was the president of the Tianjin Financial Bureau and the president of the Tianjin Merchandise Inspection Bureau. While he was very busy, my father maintained as his personal motto - "As for me and my house, we will serve the Lord." Despite the burden of business activities, he continued as chief elder in our church, serving the Lord's servants as well. Following my father like his shadow, I could see he was dredging the sewers of the church with his own hands to save money. When the roof of the church needed to be repaired, he climbed up with the builders. They worked together in order to avoid shoddy work and the use of inferior materials.

Almost every morning before office hours he enjoyed taking his chauffeur for a good breakfast. My father told him, "God created all people to be equal, whether a chauffeur or president." He was always humble and kind to his junior cadre especially being extra generous to the poor and lowly ones. He told me, "Your daddy was an extremely poor boy, never able to afford to go to school until missionaries came to China. It was truly a miracle from God sending me to a private Christian school for boys, Huiwen High with the help of the missionaries. God gave me courage and enabled me to succeed. By His grace your daddy achieved many things. I never forget I am unworthy to be a high ranking officer. I came from empty hands. So I love to help the poor and hardworking people to know

God. Only He can make their dreams come true."

My father helped many poor needy children and young students, giving free rein to their imaginations and encouraging their gifts. The Tianjin Chinese Wesley Church choir, supported by my father, influenced many great vocalists and soloists. Among them Mr. Guang Xi Li, a famous opera star, wrote in his autobiography several pages recounting David Chang's generous contribution to the community. An example of this is my father's starting a school for the impoverished paperboys who sold The New Life Evening Post on the streets. The school offered both a free lunch and four classes: English, Chinese, Mathematics and Gym. This was their only chance to learn.

David Chang's love for these newspaper boys is very clear. He was a teacher at this school and began each day meeting with the boys and asking them these questions:

"What boys did the American President Hoover think very important?"

The boys would all shout, "Newspaper boys!"

My father continued with:

"Whom does God love most?"

The boys would all shout, "ME!"

The school also provided free uniforms and socks to these poor boys. The newspaper boys learned hymns and began to sing out on the streets, "New Life Evening Post, There is important news for you," to the tune of "This Is My Father's World." They became known for their polite behavior as well-educated youngsters. Their beautiful hymn-inspired melody filled the streets. The customers began to notice the change in these boys and often gave them tips as appreciation for their singing. These boys came to call my father "Daddy Chang." Sadly, when the Communist government took over the newspaper in 1954, my father was kicked out and the school closed.

The positions of power my father held would have given many

opportunities for corruption and bribery. Many said he could be a millionaire, for he was a knowledgeable person, and the Financial Bureau and Merchandise Inspection Bureau was a sea of opportunities for grabbing money through dirty deals. Because he was always accountable to God and was not greedy, he did not become wealthy. God was always with him helping him to be clean, honest, and upright. Even when the Communist Public Security Bureau framed the case and brought false accusations against him, they could not find any wrongdoing or crime against him. They only maligned him as an American spy and counterrevolutionary Christian. Only for this reason, he was in and out of jail for 24 years. At one point when he suffered heart failure, with almost no pulse, the police took him back home, saying because he was not sentenced yet, he could not die in jail.

When he was at home he could only lie on the floor. The police would not allow us to put him on the bed, nor to send him to the hospital. No matter whether my father was lying down, or sitting, or standing up, he always prayed with love and forgiveness to everyone, including the government who wrongly mistreated him. My father was always joyful too, even when we asked him, "Father, when will we see God's justice?" He told us, "Let's read the Bible, Psalm 37 and 73." Daddy believed that every word in the Bible is true.

To our surprise, when the police found out my father had almost recovered they arrested him again. My father was in jail for another year when his heart failed once more. Then the police sent him back home. When he was almost recovered, the police returned him to the jail until 1976 when Mao Tse Dong died. Then finally came his release from jail.

Daddy recounted to me many times the story of Joseph in the Old Testament using him as our good example. God helped my father as he helped Joseph, whether in disgrace, in prison, or physically weak, to know that God can bring good out of any situation. I praise the Lord for my father's spiritual life, witnessing by his daily walk to the power, grace and mercy of the Lord Jesus.

My time in New York City

Working as a babysitter in New York City

I was chef for a day in New York City

I lost my eyesight while in New York, but the Lord healed me

Chapter XVI

Why I Went to New York

As a medical scholar I was granted a J-1 visa for one year to complete the project of Exchanging Visiting of Medical Experts and Hospitals between China and America. With this project now completed, I had to return to China, as my visa would expire. I went to New York to apply for a different kind of visa enabling me to do full-time ministry work. This required an R-1 visa. The first step was get a waiver from the J-1 visa to the R-1 before it expired. At that time there was no immigration attorney in Chapel Hill, N. C.

Whom am I supposed to ask for help? Nobody! I had a schoolmate from when we both attended Beijing Medical University. Now she had an acupuncture clinic on Park Avenue in New York City. I asked for her help. She offered me a place to stay in her storage room. Two-thirds of the room was already piled up with suitcases. There was only space for a single bed. The only window was secured by iron bars. I thank her for that help, for New York is one of the most expensive cities in the U.S. One inch of land is worth one kilo of gold.

It was the winter of 1985 that I stepped from the Greyhound bus, carrying my three suitcases and one bag. Nobody helped me. The one suitcase I could not carry was full of books. I moved along by kicking it. I had to walk for a while before I could find a taxi. Finally I arrived at the doctor's address. The two doormen who stood in front of the tall apartment building on Park Avenue immediately rushed to help me. They carried my suitcases to the basement where the storage room was located. It seemed they were expecting me. They said, "The doctor is in her clinic now. She gave me the key to let you in." Then they nodded their heads to me. All of sudden, I realized it is the time to tip them. I was not prepared for that, having only two $10 bills. Having no choice, I gave them each one. They were really happy, but afterwards I tried my best to avoid them.

I went to the clinic to thank my old classmate. She said she wanted me to work for her, but without pay. For my acupressure service, the idea was for her patients' tips to be mine. During that kind of work, I found out the good tips always came from actors and actresses, not New York millionaires. I had to save every penny for the attorney fee for my visa, so I carefully watched my expenses. As there was no kitchen for me to use, I ate a lot of hot dogs and free stale bread for several months.

My God always cares for me, including my nutrition, so He surprised me with a great chance to have daily delicious, nutritious meals. How did He do this? One day, a rich lady who was our frequent patient returned to receive my acupressure service. She said to me, "You have a pair of very soft hands. Your acupressure really helped me to get rid of my wrinkles. How much are you paid?" I explained to her that my visa problems kept me from having a salary until I could get a work permit. I had to depend on the patients' tips for my living. She seemed to care about me. She asked me again, "Do you have any other professional skills?" I replied, "Only playing the piano and singing." She said, "Can you cook Chinese food?" "Yes, I can cook homemade Chinese food," I replied. She continued telling me that she wanted to help me get another part-time job with her friend who could pay cash. That job was being a chef for this family. I wanted very much to try another part-time job. It would provide me more money to pay the attorney fee, so I went for an interview.

Chapter XVII

God Made Me a Chef

Near Central Park on 83rd Street opposite an art museum, I approached a six story building. The tall house belonging to this family had an elevator. Upon my arrival I was given an extensive menu from which I was to cook all the dishes, especially the Peking duck. Thank God for giving me a quick answer for the latter, "Peking duck should be cooked in a special vertical oven, which you don't have. I can cook home-made Peking duck for you." My Lord really helped me to prepare a fancy dinner for them. Appetizer was tomato ball with potato salad in it. The first course was beef and vegetable soup, followed by the hot dishes, Peking duck and stewed fish. The desert was flan with peaches. I was hired to be their chef part time.

My work in the kitchen began, including cleaning the three big refrigerators. When I opened the freezer of one of them, I was shocked to see a big sheep head in it! I had never cooked anything like that before! Later I found out that their holy book is the Qur'an. There was one in every room. The Lord did not give me the idea to cook pork for them, which was fortunate as they were Muslims.

Every morning I was expected to prepare the breakfast at 7:30, but they came down for breakfast at 10:30. Lunch was supposed to be served at one o'clock, but they came in around 3:00 pm. Dinner should be on at 7:30 p.m., but many times they called me to say that they would not be back for dinner. They still wanted me to wait for them, so I would rest on the sofa. When the family arrived with guests at midnight wanting to have a late dinner for over 20 people, I realized I would not have any life of my own. Even the storage room seemed like being back in jail.

I discovered that New York City is not the safest place when I had a most unfortunate experience. During the short break on Sunday from morning to 3:00 p.m. every week I used to go to church and the library, or to go to the attorney's office. One day after I had just borrowed several books from the New York City Library, I put my purse on my shoulder. Holding the books with both hands I walked down the street. Suddenly a black man bumped me. As all of the books fell to the ground he grabbed my purse from my shoulder and ran off. I cried out to those people who passed me, "Please help me! That guy stole my purse!" But nobody even looked at me. Then a policeman on horseback passed by me. I cried out the same thing to him. Stopping immediately, but very briefly, after he heard my story, he said, "If you did not get hurt, you can check out all the trash cans by yourself. This guy only wanted money. He will throw your purse into the trash can." That thief disappeared. I did not get my purse back, even after walking a long time around the streets checking the trash cans one by one. Later, a woman told me, "Walking in New York you should not carry your purse on your shoulder. You must put it into a very big bag. That will be safer." But I lost my address book, my reading glasses and my house keys.

Chapter XVIII

God Provides Me a Penthouse

One day I was told I needed to move out from the iron-barred storage room. The doctor needed it for her servant. Immediately I boldly replied I would move out in one week. "Oh, Lord!" I called out for help through my tears. When I left the clinic I walked the streets wondering what would become of me. Where was I to go? I could not afford another place and I needed to move in a week. My prayers were answered very quickly in a most amazing way.

The mistress of the family I was cooking for asked to speak with me only days after I had been asked to move. She told me that the nanny they had for their two young children needed to return to her home country of the Philippines for one month. Not wanting to hire a stranger for that time, she asked if I would be willing to take over the care of the children and live in for a month starting next week. I knew and liked the children, a one-year old baby boy and a five-year-old girl.

What a wonderful answer to my prayer! I explained to the mother that I would have to give up my job at the acupuncture clinic if I were to take on this full-time responsibility as chef and nanny. The mistress of the house responded with this offer: $1,000 per month salary and full room and board for free. I would be living in the top floor penthouse with its colorful stained glass ceiling!

One month later the nanny returned. I continued to help with the children which gave me great pleasure as I was missing my own boys so much. My employers requested me to be their full-time chef, not only cooking for the family but all of the servants. This included a secretary, laundress, nanny, house girl, cleaning boy, and me! I only discovered the huge wealth of this family when I saw their picture on the cover of the New Yorker magazine some months later.

Chapter XIX

Two Different Legal Views

I must say I already experienced many miracles from the Lord right in the midst of hardship and frustration. The whole reason I came to New York in the first place was to find an attorney expert in immigration law. I knew no one. Although there were many advertisements for such a need, I had no idea how to choose one. After praying, I closed my eyes, touching the big advertisement column in the newspaper with my index finger. My finger was on the center of a big eye-catching ad, so I went to see this immigration expert. He charged clients a very high price: first time consultancy of 30 minutes, cost $100 in cash, and that was in 1985 dollars! When my turn came, I entered and talked with this attorney for only five minutes before he told me: "I can't take your case; all the Chinese medical scholars who had a J-1 visa must return to China on time." He pointed out that coming to the U.S. for the medical field I could not then change to be in the religious field. "Your case is hopeless." He gave me back all my papers in an impolite way.

Very upset and about to leave, I was drawn over by the secretary of the attorney, Miss Wu. She had taken notes during my interview. She said: "Miss Chang, would you please come to my office? I want to talk to you." I was hopeful of getting a partial refund after the attorney took only five minutes to tell me my case was hopeless. I wondered if the secretary planned to take up the remainder of my 25 minutes. I certainly did not want to waste my time for nothing. But she insisted, so I followed her. In her office, she said to me: "Your plea touched me greatly. I graduated from Taiwan Theological Seminary, but I came to U.S. When I did not get a chance to serve the Lord full time, I changed my career to be a student in Law School. Now I am an intern working here. Why do you insist on giving up your promising career working for WHO, to be a full-time servant of God? If you are sure, I want to help you." Miss Wu agreed to take my case. And my job was to await her answer.

Chapter XX

A Burglary

This family for whom I worked loved to travel, often taking vacations on a weekend. I was the only one left in the house at night, although they had another three servants plus a secretary named Marilynn who stayed during the day. One Friday when this family left for the beach, I took the whole day to clean the refrigerator and kitchen. I didn't get a chance to go upstairs to rest until almost 5:00 p.m. As I entered my sixth floor bedroom I was horrified to discover my mattress turned inside out and my suitcases opened. Everything was strewn around my room and other rooms as well. The stained glass skylight was broken. Clearly there had been a burglar in the house. I knew Marilynn had not gone home yet, so I used the upstairs phone to tell her the shocking news.

Marilynn was as scared as I was. We immediately called the police station. They asked our address, phone number, and if anyone was hurt. They promised to send over a police officer but no one came until the next day. Worried that the homeowners might have lost some valuables, Marilynn and I foolishly took kitchen knives and two flashlights, and searched through every corner of every room of the six story house. Looking back on this I am very glad to say that we did not find any burglars still lurking in the shadows.

Marilynn said: "They won't lose anything, for I know they keep all their valuables in the bank." She thought to ask me, "What have you lost?" Poor me! I lost some jewelry, but even worse, several thousand dollars saved up in order to pay the attorney fee. No wonder when I told our mistress all about this accident by phone, she responded in a very calm voice: "Don't worry about it, we don't need to come back now, we will return on schedule."

That night I slept alone in this big house but I kept all the lights on. I prayed: "My dear Lord, what shall I do? How could I save that much money again? I know You care about me, but why am I still suffering? Please dear Lord, help me." The case remains unresolved even now. Several days later, when the family returned they never even asked me about the details of the burglary. They did not mention helping me with this disastrous loss. As I prayed my Lord granted me special peace. He kept reminding me: "Don't be afraid, just trust in Me!" The only thing I could do was "wait and see."

A couple of days later I met the rude attorney on the way to Miss Wu's office. I told him I could not pay Miss Wu the fee because of the burglary. The rude attorney upon hearing the circumstances of the burglary gave me a big smile, "You must come to my office, you know you have a strong case to sue your employer. According to law every fancy house must have its alarm system connected to the police station. That night if you had been killed it would have been your employer's fault. You can sue him for two million dollars. I would love to help you. I would just take ten percent from the settlement." I refused to do that because all my savings were lost not because of my boss, but because of the thieves. I just hoped my employer would pay me back what I lost. That's all.

Two weeks later, my employer talked to me in a very pleasant mood, saying, "Now I know you are a nice, honest, decent lady. Your God told me I have to pay you back all you lost now. Thank you so much for caring about my house and not suing me." He gave me a big check which covered everything I had lost. He also raised my salary, room and board free, plus $1200 per month. Later, I learned to my great surprise and horror that there were dirty deals among bad gangs in New York City. They bribed the servants of the rich people giving the gangs chances to burglarize them. The servants then must pretend to be burglarized too, so they could share in the booty. The servants could also sue their employers as well! I was so naive in so many ways, and thankful to be so.

Oh, my Lord, now I fully understand why my employer had observed me. But you are a miracle maker plus a professor to your children: "Be holy, be kind and be faithful by using all kinds of hardship and temptations." Being your servant I must have the wisdom to see everything from Your will, not my own will. Because *"... we know that in all things God works for the good of those who love him, who have been called according his purpose."* (Romans 8:28).

Chapter XXI

Grumbling Begets Glaucoma

Waiting for several months with no answer about the visa, I began to complain bitterly to the Lord. Freddie called me to tell me more bad news, that the American Consulate refused my whole family coming to U.S to visit me for the second time. That day was my worst day. My spirit was so low. I asked my Lord: "Is it your will? I miss my family to death! I have not seen them for three and a half long years! Will you allow me to go home?" I clearly had more lessons to learn about patience.

That very night, at midnight I was awakened by the sharpest pain in both of my eyes. My pillows were very wet by the liquids from both eyes. I became totally blind and I knew I must suffer from glaucoma! Even though I could not see, I felt my way around, put my clothes on, took the elevator, and rushed out to call a taxi. The taxi came very soon and I asked the driver to take me to the emergency room of any hospital. The driver kindly helped me get in the taxi and drove me to the Emergency Room of Bellevue Hospital. Still in great pain, I had to wait until the next morning because there was no eye doctor in the Emergency Room. I was desperate with only prayer to help me through the long night. "My Savior, you are my refuge; you are my present help in all kinds of trouble. I want to see again." Before, I remembered to "wait and see" but now I was waiting and could not see. I was blind.

Early the next morning, the eye doctor came to see me but at that time I was totally blind, experiencing both dizziness and vomiting.

He checked me out, my eye pressure on the left one was 40, on the right one 52. He told me he must take me to the operating room immediately for the surgery, but I told him I had no money with me, only 30 dollars. He maintained he didn't care if I had money or not. He had to save my eyes. So I was sent to the OR. After about two hours, with my eyes bound heavily, the world became darker. The doctor told me my left eye was fine now, but the right one cannot be healed totally. Then they sent me to the ward.

The ward seemed very noisy to me. Two other women, patients in the same room, asked me: "Hi! What is your problem?" The voice sounded like a very old woman. I told her I had eye surgery. I could not sleep very well as the other two women continued to chat noisily. A couple of hours later, a man came to my bedside and talked with me, asking how much money I had. I told him I had 30 dollars in my pocket, but $2000 cash for the flight ticket I had to go back to China. He told me I was qualified to have Medicaid. I had three months Medicaid which covered all of the costs of my surgery and one week of hospitalization. I thank God in all of these circumstances, for all things I endured were under His will; I am always in His hand as well. I never knew the social welfare system in the U.S. was so good. Before I checked out of the hospital, I could tell that the other two women patients were homeless. They got free Medicaid help too. Even they could have the nurse's special service. There were two big TV sets in that spacious ward with four beds. The hospital treated all the patients ---whether criminals, guarded by police, the homeless or the poor--- very well and with great care. There is no place in the world where the traveler or visitor is treated with such mercy and kindness. I experienced this as a Chinese scholar with a pending visa.

I must give thanks to the Lord for leading me to the family who employed me. They allowed me to have rest in their home without serving them during my time of convalescence. Also I thank God for healing me through the good doctor's hands. I remember one of the interns especially, Dr. Snow, who showed great compassion and gentleness while I was at the hospital. My Lord also healed the wounds in my heart. He kept giving me the songs which I loved so much. The titles of the songs are "He Lives," "His Eye Is on The Sparrow," and especially, "Amazing Grace," --"I once was lost, but now am found, Was blind but now I see."

I realized I have to obey His will to be his witness no matter how long I have to wait for my family reunion. I asked my Lord for forgiveness because I was not faithful to Him. So many times, my heart was willing, but my flesh was weak. My blind right eye is a mark of my weak faith being shaken countless times.

One day, Miss Wu called me, eight long months after she took my case. She said, "Congratulations! You won the case! The agreement between Chinese and American governments regarding the medical scholars having to return to China changed such that public health which is what you studied at UNC is not covered. You can get a work permit and your waiver. Please come to my office to know the details. But now I must tell you our God is really helping you." I thanked her and shouted "Alleluia! Alleluia!" My Lord is omnipotent and omniscient! He alone is wonderful!

Chapter XXII

Music and Museums

I do not want you to think suffering was the only kind of experience I had during my adventures in New York. My life there also had some very happy times. Every Sunday I went to Calvary Baptist Church. This is a large church with a very professional choir. I met a good Chinese Christian, a little bit older than I, Miss Lillion Lu. When she discovered I had a good voice, she suggested I join the choir to serve the Lord. She showed me an announcement that they needed a first soprano. Despite their very tough examination, I decided to try out. They required the choir members not only sing and read music, but also know how to play another instrument. The strict conductor listened to my singing and piano playing and also gave me a music sheet to test my reading. Thank God I was accepted. Serving the Lord in that choir, I was so blessed once again to be a part of a group singing praises to God.

Loving classical music very much, when I got free time from my employer, I enjoyed going to Lincoln Center for its wonderful programs. The first time I went, I found the tickets to be quite expensive. I could only afford a seat so high up and far from the stage, it was difficult to hear and see very much of anything. But I found out a lot of rich people who dressed elegantly, left after the first section, no matter the opera, symphony or ballet. Most of them lived on Long Island so had a great distance to get home. So I went to talk to them: "Do you come back?" They answer "No." I told them I was eager to listen to this opera, may I have your tickets?

Elegantly dressed as I was, they kindly gave me their tickets. So I was able to enjoy many popular operas, even if only from the second half--Aida, Madame Butterfly--Tchaikovsky symphonies, and Swan Lake, Sleeping Beauty ballets at Lincoln Center. Mind you, only for the second section but free and in a good seat! That was good enough for me. See, my Lord also knows how to make me happy. Only He alone!

Entries to local museums were within my budget, so I often delighted myself with strolling through the galleries. So many huge oil paintings drew me to contemplate them for hours. I particularly liked the Old Masters, although modern art still eludes my understanding. I was certainly drawn to the paintings representing the Old Testament scenes and characters. The landscapes and paintings of beautiful people soothed my soul in those days in New York City.

Central Park and the City Library were other places I frequented in my limited free time. These places offered me opportunities to learn and take advantage of where God had put me, although I never stopped missing my husband and twin sons. The Lord knew how to comfort me despite the aching in my heart for my loved ones still so far away in China. Sometimes I asked God why I had to experience this unbearable loneliness. Much later I discovered the answer to that question.

Chapter XXIII

He Made My Cup Overflow

October 1988 brought the nearly five years of waiting for our family reunion to an end. My husband Freddie and my twin sons, Joseph and Daniel, finally came to the United States of America. The first thing we did was to give thanks to God, taking our boys to worship our Lord at the Covenant Church of God near our place at Pen Park Lane. It was there that Pastor Bare baptized our two sons.

Joseph and Daniel worked very hard in their high school, both graduating as outstanding honor students. They also helped Freddie and me with housekeeping, as well as serving the Lord in our Chinese church. For five years it was a Chinese Christian Bible Study fellowship, later maturing into our Chinese church. I was so happy to see my two sons loving the Lord, and loving people with their kind hearts. Sometimes they helped Chinese students and scholars to learn how to drive, as well as with cooking, shopping, and moving. The boys knew our family daily food was always very simple, but they never complained. Every Friday night would be a bit different. After Bible study time we would have fancy meals for all the fellowship people at our home.

Prior to my having my R-1 visa, returning to China and possibly not being able to come back to the United States was a real fear. Once I had my green card, the permanent resident status, I could go back and forth to China safely. In 1990 Freddie and I started to minister in China. We contacted some of my old church friends who suffered many years in jail for their faith as we both had. Bible study groups and house churches sprang up like bamboo shoots, developing so fast that the hunger for God was palpable. Freddie also helped me with the office work, traveling to many states to give testimonies, share the vision and raising support for the fledgling churches in China.

Dr. Bob Finley, founder of Christian Aid Mission, ordained us to be missionaries. This was the greatest honor for us. Chairman Jeffrey Shaw prayed for us as he oversaw the ceremony. Afterwards we started to go to China every year to support house churches, Bible study groups and to build the network of Chinese indigenous ministries. Only our Lord loves to use the unworthy broken vessels who love Him wholeheartedly to serve Him. Every year, Freddie and I could see clearly the revival wave of Chinese house churches was led by Christ Jesus alone. He always did and continues to do new things, every year. We marveled at the new developments. More and more Chinese people who never knew Jesus or the Bible had zeal to know Jesus and to be baptized through our coworkers' love and teaching. They all understood they were sinners. They confessed their sins with tears and accepted the Lord Jesus sincerely as their own Savior.

Many coworkers joyfully dedicated their lives in the field for Christ Jesus. These new believers are truly the fruit of the work done over many years by the first missionaries in the early 1900s. They came so far from their homes to share the love of God with the Chinese people. We were seeing the third generation of the first fruit of these missionaries. I am one of those of the third generation and my sons are the fourth generation.

Networks of indigenous missions rapidly grew, all led by our Lord. Before, the revival was in the rural areas but now even in the cities there are many registered churches. The independent churches now in the big cities have in their congregations intellectuals, college students, professors, musicians, artists, and white collar workers. The independent churches are registered with the government, but their senior pastors were not sent by the Three Self Patriotic organization. The pastors are overseas Chinese pastors who returned to China or Taiwanese businessmen who are laymen, but leading the churches. Even I was so surprised! So how did this explosion happen? Only Him, my Lord!

◆ HE ALONE ◆

Chapter XXIV

God Opens Even More Doors

We went to Taiwan in 1996 to raise support for Chinese indigenous ministries in China. The Lord blessed us by leading us to Pastor James Shia and Mrs. Shia. They are faithful, creative, gifted servants of God who planted "The Gospel Movement of the 20th Century," which became known as "The Chinese Christian Evangelical Association" (CCEA). They gave us tremendous help being a good example for all the missionaries to follow. From then on we visited Taiwan working with CCEA and traveled over the whole island to share our ministries and raise support. All the staff of CCEA had compelled us to serve the Lord with more wisdom, more zeal, and more strategically. Going to Taiwan every year, we see by our own eyes the Constitution of the Republic of China is built upon democracy and the respecting of human rights. This year President Ma continuing his presidency is an obvious event to prove their election was held in a free and democratic way. The founding father of ROC, Mr. Yit-Shian Sun and his "Three People's Principles" -- Nationalism, Democracy and People's Livelihood is similar to the principles of the American government -- "Of the people, by the people, and for the people."

In 2007 Freddie and I were invited to preach at a church in the headquarters of the Nationalist Party. This would be the equivalent of being asked to preach in a church located in the heart of our nation's seat of power in Washington, D.C.!

God Calls Me to Many Other Countries

I had many chances to visit countries in South America, like Argentina, Brazil and also Costa Rica - as well as Puerto Rico, and Southeast Asia, including Singapore, the Philippines, Malaysia and Indonesia, through Christian Aid offices. In those countries and places I preached at many, many churches. Churches gave me a warm welcome and most of the congregations numbered more than 2,000 people. A lot of people welcomed my testimony and my book, *Clay in the Potter's Hand*. Countless numbers of people were baptized during my visits, and the Lord's name was glorified as He should be. Filled with the Holy Spirit, I felt anointed by the Lord to preach His Word. The congregations were touched and uplifted by the same Holy Spirit. The congregations gave me a nickname - La China - Chinese face but a Latin heart! God alone has made me a missionary.

One humorous moment in my travels for the Lord came when I had the opportunity to preach at a Chinese Christian church in Wantirna, Victoria, Australia in 2002. As I was speaking, I could not help but notice a man sitting in the front row of the church. He was making funny faces at me and slightly waving his hand. Unbelievably, it turned out to be a man with whom I had attended Sunday School and kindergarten in Tianjiang YWCA in China in 1938! Sitting next to this man, Winston Xue, who was certainly the naughtiest boy in kindergarten, was another nice-looking gentleman who stared at me while sporting a big smile on his face. He was another classmate of ours at the same kindergarten and Sunday School. William Liang was the leader of our class so many years ago in China. They were both there with their lovely wives. This was an incredible surprise as we had not seen each other for many long years. The reunion in Australia was wonderful for all of us, as well as being a part of God's plan to help me at a later time. Prior to Winston's relocating to Australia, he was the Vice-President of the Tianjiang television station. He was popular and had a busy social life, as he traveled in and out of China often. He had this mobility because he had become a Communist Party member, allowing him to meet many VIPs. After he moved to Australia, Winston, as well as William Liang, regained their faith in Christ. Winston and his wife, Shuan, kept up with Freddie and me after this initial reunion, including a visit with us for his 80th birthday journey to reunite with friends in the U.S. Our time in Australia was delightfully filled with many times of reunions with these classmates from my childhood.

My Lord also led me to Canada where there was another Christian Aid office in Fort Erie. That became independent from Christian Aid, changing the title to Intercede International in 2007. President James Eagle helped me and Freddie over many years to extend our church visiting in Canada. We continue to be grateful for the financial and prayer support we receive from Canadian Churches. I am very thankful to God for James and his wife, Sharon, and the office staff and donors.

Chapter XXV

Walking Where Jesus Walked

My dream to go to Israel to walk where Jesus walked is something that I prayed for over many years. Not having enough money for the travel fee delayed this dream coming true. Finally, I joined a travel group with close friends, Mr. and Mrs. Greg and Carolyn Phillips, Pastor and Mrs. Bruce and Vicky Johnson, and several others. Like the disciples, we numbered twelve in the group. An adventure of a lifetime, this exciting journey included spiritual filling, crying, laughter and praise! Wherever I walked in Jerusalem, at the Sea of Galilee, in the City of David, St. Peter's Church, Capernaum, or the Mount of Beatitudes, I strongly felt the presence of God.

Visiting with a community of Messianic Jews was another amazing experience. A highlight of our trip was at the Jordan River where Freddie and I were both rededicated with Pastor Bruce presenting us once again to our Heavenly Father. When Pastor Bruce put me in the Jordan River, for just a second I felt I had died with my Lord. Coming up out from the water, the peace and the joy I had was impossible to describe! I felt as if I were flying! It was as if the Lord Himself baptized me with blood and water.

When our group was sailing on the Sea of Galilee I prayed during our worship time, "Thank you, Lord, for this boat. Here are all your servants and children. Please strengthen our faith, enable us to serve you better. Once, your disciples experienced your words being able to calm the storm. Thank you so much for giving us many storms in our lives to train our faith. You complete our faith by the same power to calm the storms in our lives. We praise you, the King of Kings, and Lord of Lords!"

When I visited the Park of Gethsemane I saw the big rock where my Lord kneeled down to pray with tears and sweat like drops of blood. Nearby I saw the huge nearly thousand-year-old fig trees splitting, but held together by strong chains. Still, the new branches were visible. At Cana we had a golden wedding anniversary of Pastor Bruce and Vicky Johnson. That was another highlight of our trip. Only my Lord understands my heart, how much I want to follow in His footsteps. He made my dream come true. He was so close to me every minute of my visit to Israel. During the ten days traveling in Israel I sang almost every day the song I love most: "I Walked Today Where Jesus Walked." The lyrics tell exactly how I felt as my tears of gratitude silently fell.

Freddie and I rededicated our lives in the Jordan River with pastor Bruce Johnson

Chapter XXVI

Becoming an American Citizen

Monticello, the home of Thomas Jefferson, author of the Declaration of Independence, is the special place where I had the honor of becoming an American citizen. On that day, July 4th, 1996 there were about 200 new citizens taking the oath with me. The people presiding over the naturalization ceremony were high ranking officials of the city government. They chose several delegates representing their former countries to give a one minute remark after taking the oath of allegiance. I was chosen to represent China sharing my feelings as a citizen of my new country.

"Excuse me? Only one minute? What shall I say? Lord, you've got to teach me how to give a one minute remark totally expressing my feelings." Each one of several other delegates finished their remarks which were more than one minute. Some talked about the freedom and human rights available to them today, about being able to do anything they want, about dreams coming true for them. The congregation gave every one of them welcome applause after they spoke.

When I went up the many stairs to the huge porch of the stately red brick former home of the third President of the United States, I still didn't know what I was going to say. I was the last one to speak. The applause from the previous speaker had died down when I got to the top. When I reached the lectern, all of a sudden the words came out from my heart, and into the silence, I shouted, "Praise the Lord!" Although there were 800 visitors seated there, it was so quiet you could have heard a pin drop on the ground. The words just rushed out of me, "Today is my honor day to be an American citizen. Why did I apply to be a U.S. citizen? Because I knew there is only one great nation under God, the United States of America, and her constitution was established based on fearing God. My father, a returned Chinese scholar of America, told me, "Someday you must go to America to learn the wonderful spirit of their constitution, because our God blessed this country, and this people with that. You can see each new President of the U.S. must put his left hand on the Bible, and the last words of the Presidential Inauguration is, 'So help me God.' And you also can see there are four words printed on the one dollar bill, 'In God we trust.' Their national anthem and spiritual songs like 'God Bless America,' 'God of our Fathers' are full of the words of praising God. Now I believe what the Bible says: *'Blessed is the nation whose God is the Lord...'* (Psalm 33: 12). I want to be a better citizen. From now on I must pray for my country, the United States of America, earnestly to keep on the right track because without fearing God our nation and our people wouldn't be blessed. May God bless America."

My one minute remark finished, I stepped down to go back to my seat. I didn't hear any applause. It was so still, so quiet. I thought maybe they didn't understand my Chinese-accented English. Before I sat down, everybody suddenly stood up, the applause like a thunderstorm! The conductor of the band ran over to me, saying, "We don't know each other, but thank you so much for giving us these wonderful words." Then he ran back to the band, leading them in a thrilling rendition of "God Bless America." Immediately the whole place and atmosphere erupted as everyone began to sing those rousing lyrics. Reporters, journalists, and people surrounded me as they gave me their fervent greetings and warm hugs.

I left for Canada to see my baby sister Grace after the ceremony. Two days later when I came back to my place a lot of cards and letters were in my mailbox. All of the cards were giving me thanks for what I had said. Somebody wrote, "Your remarks made me thrilled, I felt honored again to be an American." Our church people told me that the whole ceremony of my naturalization was on the air on TV. However, the Daily Progress newspaper reports of my remarks were sadly missing "under God" which is how I had described my new country. But I am so thankful and honored to be the citizen of God's Kingdom. Only my Lord's precious blood made me a child of God, which is an honor higher than any the world could ever give me.

When I sing the national anthem for my new country, I always appreciate especially the fourth stanza, which is seldom remembered these days, it seems. Here is a reminder, as written by Frances Scott Key, in 1814, the fourth stanza of the Star-Spangled Banner:

O thus be it ever when freemen shall stand
Between their lov'd home and the war's desolation!
Blest with vict'ry and peace may the heav'n rescued land
Praise the power that hath made and preserv'd us a nation!
Then conquer we must, when our cause it is just,
And this be our motto - "In God is our trust,"
And the star-spangled banner in triumph shall wave
O'er the land of the free and the home of the brave.

Becoming a new American citizen, giving my speech

Becoming a new American citizen, with my family

Chapter XXVII

Winter and Summer Rescues

Clay in the Potter's Hand includes stories of the 20 long years I spent, falsely accused, in forced hard labor camps and jail in China. My death could easily have come during those years through beatings, starvation, mass violence, or sheer exhaustion, to name a few of the hardships I endured. God evidently had other plans for me, for without my Savior's ever present help I would have died a long, long time ago.

My missionary life, this Christian's life in America, is more comfortable and easier, especially enjoying being loved here and people accepting my love as well. I began to volunteer in the Christian community as soon as I arrived in the U.S. I traveled many miles in 1984 helping different ministries between Raleigh, Durham, Cary and Chapel Hill. One day when I had just gotten my driver's license, three months after coming to America, I drove to The Good News For All Nations (TGNFAN) TV station in Raleigh, NC. For that I had to drive back and forth from Chapel Hill to Raleigh every Tuesday from 9 p.m. to 11 p.m. With the program over around 10:30 p.m., I was on the way back to Chapel Hill when a snow storm hit. The snow became heavier and heavier. I had driven the car only two or three miles when I couldn't see the lines on the road anymore. The snow storm continued to rage.

I decided naively, and rather foolishly, to stop the car, lock myself in, and sleep. I thought the people would plow the highway by the next morning when I could then drive back. It was so cold.

I just tried to close my eyes. I could not get to sleep and the snow heavily covered my car. I was just an like Eskimo living in an ice cave.

American policemen are so different from Chinese policemen. I thank God for sending me an especially nice policeman. He cleared the snow from my car windows and used his flashlight to check inside. He spotted me in the back seat. He knocked firmly on the window. "What are you doing here?" he wanted to know. I explained about being a new driver, the snow being too heavy, and my not being able to see the line on the road. The kind policeman told me I would freeze to death if I stayed there. He gave me instructions to follow, beginning with warming up the engine for at least five minutes, my two hands only holding the wheel, that his car would pull my car out driving back slowly. With a heavy chain connecting our two vehicles, he pulled me all the way back to my place. On that bitter cold night, this caring policeman spent over an hour seeing me safely home. I was so grateful I asked him to come in to have a hot chocolate and warm up a little bit. He refused me in a very polite way, "Madame, I am on duty, but thank you so much."

I told him: "You are my angel tonight."

He replied, "This is my job. Good night! " He left after I asked for his card. The very next day I wrote a thank you card to his station telling the whole story of his good service. Without this policeman rescuing me, I surely would have frozen to death in the car. What a great country, where people are so kind and decent. I thought my Lord must have laughed at my stupid plans, so He sent the nice policeman to rescue me immediately. Only He, my Savior, was watching over me all the time.

In the summer of 2004, I had a speaking engagement in Austin, Texas. When I reached there both of my legs were badly swollen causing sharp pain. But I thought it doesn't matter, after the Sunday service I will go home. Sunday morning the swelling and pain worsened. I prayed, "Lord, help me to finish what you want me to say." When the service was over, I could not even move.

Some people sent me to the hospital emergency room. There a doctor found out I suffered deep vein thrombosis, a serious condition. I was sent to the ward and told I needed surgery. I asked the doctor, "Could you give me some blood thinner allowing me to go home right away. I have no family and no friends here. I was only a speaker in the church."

The doctor said, "Yes, if you sign your name on the check-out form, you will take all the responsibility. You might die on the airplane as your blood is too thick." I knew how to administer the blood thinner myself, so I felt a peace, as I willingly checked out of the hospital. On the plane I gave myself a shot of Warfarin to thin my blood. When I reached Charlottesville, a brother in Christ in our Chinese church, Dr. Ming-Cheng Shih, a visiting scholar in the Vascular Department of UVA Hospital, visited me. Discovering my physical problem, he insisted I go to the Emergency Room of UVA. He told me, "Dorothy, you need surgery as soon as possible." He checked my lab report, blood test, INR and PTT was 0.1.

I truly thank God for him. Because he was working in that department, I was hospitalized immediately, while he booked me for surgery early the next morning. After the six a.m. surgery, the doctor told me,"You had very bad blood clots in both legs. The blood clots in some vessels were sucked out, but your lower left leg was not totally cleaned. Additionally, when we did the surgery, we found out you had a very big blood clot under your heart. We thought we had to take this clot out first, but it was too near your heart."

After conferring with my husband, Freddie, they performed another surgery to suck out the big blood clot near my heart. This was a dangerous procedure with a 50% possibility of my not surviving the operation. The surgery was successful. The big clot was totally removed. They put two stents in my blood vessels. When the doctor asked me whether I had done any hard labor, or possibly been struck by something heavy, I said no. It took me a while to recall that from

1960 to 1980, I was always pressed by the heavy iron hinges and hardware boxes, weighing more than 80 pounds each. Lifting these, moving them from the workshop to the big storage hall, they were so heavy I had to place them on my stomach in order to hold them. My prison hard labor included piling them up one by one for at least 10 hours per day during ten long years. See, the Lord already protected me, even when those blood clots had already filled my leg blood vessels. He stopped the big blood clots from going into my heart by sticking them on bigger vessels under the heart. If the blood clots had gone into my heart, I would have died instantly! I didn't know what He had done to rescue me when I was experiencing the life-threatening disease of deep vein thrombosis. Only He is my Savior!

Chapter XXVIII

Why I Am Still Alive

Freddie and I attended a New Year's party for church members in 2006. Freddie enjoyed some wine. On our way home Freddie lost the way. We were driving not knowing where we were going. No highway, no light, and no houses in sight, and it was raining. When Freddie made a quick left U-turn, the right side of the car where I was sitting bumped into a big tree. Then the car fell into a pit. Glass from the front and the right side windows broke everywhere, and shards from them filled my mouth. Warm blood spurted from my injured head. I later learned from the doctor I had broken my breast bone, seven ribs, and the third and fourth spinal cords were fractured. The severe pain, bleeding head and mouth, along with all of the broken bones made it impossible to move at all. Freddie was on the driver side, so he had not been hurt. Because I was taking the blood thinner daily, the bleeding was even more abundant. I shouted urgently to Freddie, "Hit the horn!" Then I just passed out. To make matters worse, we did not have a cell phone. Nobody knew our critical situation. But our Lord knows all things. Later I learned God sent an old couple who heard the sound of our horn. They boldly drove to where we were and used their cell phone to call 911.

The car accident happened around 10:50 p.m. I lost consciousness until 1:20 a.m. the next day. Doctors fixing my fractured head bones with pins awakened me with a violent, sharp pain. I thought perhaps my Lord was coming to get me, but my beautiful, wonderful, incredible dream was rudely interrupted. I would have preferred to stay in the pain-free place. Was it a dream or a vision? Or was it true? Before I woke up I was lying on a warm, thick and solid palm bed in a very pleasant light, not a room, nor a tunnel, just an indescribably bright place. So when I was shocked back to consciousness, I wanted to return to the beautiful light and enjoyment of that comfortable warm palm bed. Friend, I don't care if you believe it or not, I believe that was my Lord. He alone can do everything to help His children. *"Even though I walk through the valley of the shadow of death, I will fear no evil, for you are with me..."* Psalm 23: 4. I also believe that heaven will be much more beautiful than the bright place which I so briefly experienced.

I believe that was a serious lesson for us. Freddie should not have been drinking wine, and then insisting to drive, refusing the advice of others. But why did the accident happen? Why did the Lord not protect me in the first place? I believe that when we choose to do things outside of His will, God does use all kinds of methods to remind His children of what we must and must not do. I think this accident happened to teach us some important lessons. First, Freddie should not have drunk the wine. Second, the Lord let me experience His great love, which is much, much deeper than a husband's love can be. This is true no matter how good a husband one may be blessed to have.

Five days later Freddie left for China as we had done every year. He went to help with the ministries there. I supported him in this decision to go on schedule because I knew how badly they needed us. My sons and daughters-in-law all came to see me. I was hospitalized for a full month. My situation was awful. I could not lie down on the bed because of my wounds on the third and fourth spinal surgery area. I could not turn to my left or right side because both sides had ribs broken. Having my face downward was not an option as my chest bone was broken. Miraculous as it seems, the Lord protected my face from the broken glass. While the shards filled my mouth, no glass was embedded in my face, not even one small fragment, so that my appearance remained the same after my broken bones healed.

I prayed, "Lord, I know you love me so much. You trained me not to rely upon Freddie only. You know my character is too emotional, so if I love somebody I will pour out all my love to him. I required my husband to do the same thing, not to stop serving the Lord in China because of me. Then I would not ask for Your help nor have intimacy with You." So when I prayed again, "Lord, would You touch my wounds to ease my pain?" I just finished that prayer when I felt a soft hand touching me. As I opened my eyes, that was the hand of my dear sister in Christ, Mary Kong. From that moment on she helped me for one entire month during which all my wounds were totally healed. I knew that was my Lord who used a good doctor, Dr. Chris Shaffrey to help me. Even the wounds remind me very often to see God's will, God's help, God's never failing and everlasting love. This is a unique understanding that I have to know. There is no human who has that kind of love. It is critical for me to know my Lord trained me to be His servant, whose heart and emotions need totally to rely upon Him alone. Otherwise, the world or anybody else can use conditional human love that will hurt me and pull my spirit down. He wants me to give His abundant love to all of the needy ones. 2 Corinthians 1:4 - *"[Christ] comforts us in all our troubles, so that we can comfort those in any trouble with the comfort we ourselves have received from God."*

I feel great gratitude to those who took such tremendous good care of me in my severe time of need. Those at First Baptist Church, Christian Aid Mission, the Chinese Gospel Church and individual dearest ones who visited and filled my room with flowers during my recuperation period, these I so appreciate with a grateful heart.

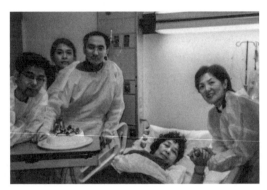

Why did I not die?

Chapter XXIX

Freddie's Going Home

Beginning in 2007 Freddie's health suffered greatly from several different cancers invading his body. During a period of six long years, he endured different treatments as he continued to serve the Lord until He took him home on August 22, 2012. Freddie was very strong, maintaining his faith despite the terrible side effects of the chemotherapy and radiation for colon, rectal, lung and brain cancer. As the cancer spread throughout his body, we continued to pray, "Let Your will be done in our lives." Freddie and I always mentioned the following two scriptures in our prayers:

"For my thoughts are not your thoughts, neither are your ways my ways," declares the Lord. Isaiah 55:8

Psalm 78:7 *"Then they would put their trust in God and would not forget his deeds but would keep his commands."*

We always asked God to give us big faith and great joy in the midst of this cancer trial. Our Lord God truly answered our appeals by giving Freddie no pain at all in six years! His appetite, energy, and ability to sleep were amazing, far different from other cancer patients suffering from the same diseases. This allowed Freddie to continue to work, to travel to China, and never did he have to ask for sick leave time. He wore his chemotherapy pack to work during his treatment and even joked about it, as he patted his stomach area. He did not even lose his hair. We praise the Lord for answering our prayers so completely.

God always has a plan for His children. By the first of June

2012 Freddie started to lose his balance and walking began to be a problem. His sight, loss of appetite and energy level deteriorated. He had trouble swallowing anything from then on. One by one, his body functions began to fail quite quickly. It was then that the doctor stopped the treatments and told me that Freddie had only two weeks to live. We moved Freddie to Hospice House at that time, but our prayer always focussed on praising our Lord for His salvation and the free gift of eternal life. If the Lord wanted to take Freddie home, we would say, "Alleluia!" If the Lord wanted to give him many more years to serve Him, we say the same "Alleluia!" because there is no death in our lives. Whether one is a king or a beggar, human beings all experience birth, growth, aging, sometimes sickness and death. As Christians we believe that the body may die, but the spirit will fall asleep waiting to be resurrected until the Lord comes again.

1 Corinthians 15:51-55 (NIV)

"Listen, I tell you a mystery: We will not all sleep, but we will all be changed — in a flash, in the twinkling of an eye, at the last trumpet. For the trumpet will sound, the dead will be raised imperishable, and we will be changed. For the perishable must clothe itself with the imperishable, and the mortal with immortality. When the perishable has been clothed with the imperishable, and the mortal with immortality, then the saying that is written will come true: 'Death has been swallowed up in victory. Where, O death, is your victory? Where, O death, is your sting?'"

1 Thessalonians 4:14-17 (NIV)

"For we believe that Jesus died and rose again, and so we believe that God will bring with Jesus those who have fallen asleep in him. According to the Lord's word, we tell you that we who are still alive, who are left until the coming of the Lord, will certainly not precede those who have fallen asleep. For the Lord himself will come down from heaven, with a loud command, with the voice of the archangel and

with the trumpet call of God, and the dead in Christ will rise
first. After that, we who are still alive and are left will be
caught up together with them in the clouds to meet the Lord
in the air. And so we will be with the Lord forever."

During the last moments of Freddie's life when he could no longer
see, he could still hear. I was embracing his head and shoulder. His
twin sons and five grandchildren were holding his hands. We sang
songs of praise for him. As we sang these words, the third verse of
Amazing Grace - "Through many dangers, toils and snares I have
already come; 'Tis Grace that brought me safe thus far and Grace
will lead me home" - Freddie peacefully and comfortably breathed
his last.

After my husband Freddie went home to be with the Lord, we
did not announce this news to many people. Even so there were over
400 people who came to his memorial service. I am very thankful to
the founder of Christian Aid Mission, Dr. Bob Finley and his wife,
Cynthia, and all of the Board Members and staff of Christian Aid
Mission. Others for whom I am thankful are the Chinese Gospel
Church family, First Baptist Church family, Mr. and Mrs. James and
Sharon Eagle, all part of Intercede International Mission and their
staff in Canada. Love poured out on me and my family from as far
as Connecticut, New Jersey, North and South Carolina, and Florida.
Many from the Chantilly Bible Church and Northern Virginia
Chinese Christian Church showed their love, help and caring words
as well as warm hugs and gifts. This touched and encouraged me
very much.

The service itself was a time of lifting up the Lord Jesus Christ,
with honor and glory as memories of how Freddie had served Him
over many years were recounted. Every praising hymn continued
with the same sonorous harmony and spirit, the same unity of heart
thanking God for the eternal life we have in Christ. We buried
Freddie's ashes in a beautiful quiet grave yard, "Garden of Devotion"
in Virginia. Senior Pastor Caleb Wang of the Taiwan Assembly of

God led the ceremony.

When everyone had gone and the perfect ceremony was over, I went back to my silent, empty home. All of a sudden, the wave of loneliness hit me and I felt an attack of deep sorrow and weariness. I felt paralyzed as I sat down on the sofa, feeling completely alone. A flood of tears rolled down my cheeks. I began to understand that now I am a widow. I murmured to my Lord, "I need You, Lord. I need You." I opened my Bible, as I was accustomed to doing. Not seeking any particular verses, my eyes immediately came to rest upon Isaiah 54:5 and 10:

> *For your Maker is your husband—*
> *the Lord Almighty is his name—* . . .
> *"Though the mountains be shaken*
> *and the hills be removed,*
> *yet my unfailing love for you will not be shaken*
> *nor my covenant of peace be removed,"*
> *says the Lord, who has compassion on you.*

These verses restored my soul as God showed His great mercy to me with a warm stream flowing through me. He wiped away my tears at that moment of great comforting. I sensed my dear Lord kept telling me, "I will hold your hands. Stand up, pressing on towards the goal. Finish the race. I will be with you to the end."

The month after Freddie's funeral I went to China to continue the ministry Freddie and I began together.

Chapter XXX

Witnesses and Martyrs Like Clouds Around Me

When I was a child the intimacy with my Lord Jesus was based on my simple little child-like faith with no understanding of the Trinity nor deep spiritual truths. I thought of the Lord as my daddy-Jesus who loved and protected me. As I grew older, the intimacy I had with the Lord became stronger. From 1936 to 1949, the government gave full freedom of religion especially to the Christians. Under the nationalist administration of President Chiang-Kai-Shek and First Lady, both Christians, I was able to join the youth evangelistic movements. Evangelistic meetings, crusades for youth, parades on the street, Christian youth disaster relief, and solid Bible studies gave me a new foundation for my faith. I began to feel that I was serving the Lord and He loved to use me in many ways.

People began to notice my zealous service for the Lord. Their response was loving and praising me. My pride was nourished and proceeded to grow quickly. I began to compare myself with other kids, paying attention to the way I dressed, the credit from my Bible study, my gift of playing the piano, singing, and being the leader of the Sunday school. Little by little worldly concerns with superficial beauty occupied me, things like fashion, social dancing, movies, and parties. From there I envied the beautiful looking movie stars and famous musicians, especially vocalists. At that time my mother was a professional soprano vocalist and I wanted to be even better than she was. Thank God He noticed my heart slowly moved towards the world, no longer satisfied to obey the instruction from the Bible.

God allowed my circumstances to change radically.

My first year of junior high, in 1949 the Communists came to power and everything changed for me and the whole country. Public education focused on atheism, and brainwashing started with the kids and youth. If anybody asked me about the conflict between creation and evolution, I did not know how to argue with them. When I went home and asked my father how to answer them, he told me to be quiet and not to argue with them. But if my Lord Jesus was maligned, I couldn't accept it. I told them I did not believe human beings came from apes. I still strongly believed that I have a heavenly Father, that my Lord Jesus created me and loves me. In school all the good students applied to be Young Pioneers Communist team members. When they were accepted, they had to say the oath to be boundlessly loyal to the Communist Party, which I did not like at all. So I did not apply. By senior high everybody applied to be a member of the Communist Youth League of China, taking exactly the same oath to the Communist Party. Very shortly all of my classmates became Young Pioneers, later becoming league members. I was the only one in my class of seventy students who did not apply to be one, even though I received good marks for my studies. I was no longer classified as a "good student," as I did not join these Communist groups. Gone were the good comments or praise from the people around me. Thank God for my parents who encouraged me to love praise from the Lord, not from people. Still I felt hurt and disgraced as my peers looked down upon me. My faith and obedience started to be challenged.

The faith and the obedience always struggled with the evaluation from people. The struggle was really with my pride. But confronting this big pressure and my chosen career to be a medical doctor, I started to ask my Lord: "I am only your young girl. How could I handle this hardship to keep my faith in You? Give up my career? Be a Christian whom people always hated?" Yet I did not know the more serious challenge to come my faith and obedience would have to go through later.

I joined the fellowship belonging to Pastor Ming-Dao Wang tabernacle when I was a medical student in Beijing Medical University. He was greatly faithful to the Lord and preached the whole Bible truth boldly. Because of this the government watched them very carefully. One day in 1957 the authorities of the University called up all the students of all the departments, professors, and personnel to go to the great hall in the campus. They used this organized meeting to accuse all the Christian students as American spies. We were forced to stand on the stage of the hall. I was one of the 46 accused Christians. Even the attendants looked surprised. One of the authorities in charge of this meeting announced that these students on the stage had long been instructed to be good medical doctors and loyal to the government. But they had made no progress on changing their belief in the foreign God and the foreign religion. Now is the final chance for them to convert to the Communist Party Chairman Mao. Some student communists came up to the stage and started to accuse us of having a secret meeting place in the backyard of the campus. They claimed we must be against Chairman Mao and The Communist Party. I was furious with their purely fictitious accusations, but I also feared what would be the next step. So I stood behind the very tall Christian brother who used to lead our prayer fellowship. He was older and his wife had just had a baby boy. As she was holding the infant, she was allowed to sit among the communist students.

The leader of the meeting announced: "We have already heard all of the accusations. We can give them the choice: to keep the dumb faith in their foreign God and wrongdoing or to totally trust in our great Chinese Communist Party and great Chairman Mao. If they make the wrong choice, they will face serious consequences. Now we give them ten seconds to make up their minds." At exactly that moment through the windows we saw the armed military soldiers and their trucks parked outside the hall. They announced again to the Christians on the stage: "You listen carefully, if you decide to come back to the people, move to the left side of the stage. If you decide to keep your God, move to the right side on the stage. We are counting the ten seconds for you." He immediately began the counting: "One…, two…, three…, four…,"

I was scared to death. Left, or right? I thought the Lord is on the right side of Almighty God in heaven now. The Lord divided the sheep and the goats, with the sheep on the right side. I knew that I was supposed to move to the right side, my God's side, but I saw more than two-thirds of our brothers and sisters moved to the left side. The crowd instantly shouted: "Welcome back to the people's side! Come down from the stage to join us!" The clapping hands of more than one thousand students sounded like thunder. The meeting leader announced: "See, the people welcome everyone to the great Communist Party, and anybody who is changeable and teachable will have a bright future. Now you see only these very few stubborn ones remaining, but we still can give them a final chance to make their decision." Then he asked our leader's wife who carried her baby boy to come to the front of the stage. This crying sister and crying baby came, but the stage was very high. She could not reach her husband's shoulder, so she held his two legs tightly, and murmured to her husband: "Would you please be smart, just move a little bit to the left, and we can trust in the Lord and keep worshiping Him at home. Otherwise you will be arrested and what shall I and your baby do then? Please!"

With my whole body shaking in fear as I hid behind this brother, I saw him standing there not looking at his wife and his baby boy at all. He was holding his head up and looking up at the ceiling. I knew that he was looking to our Lord, trying so hard to hold back his tears. His action made the authority leader very mad. He shouted again: "See how counter-revolutionary they are! They would rather love their foreign God than their wives and babies. They are inhuman! Let us count again! Give the rest of the stubborn ones ten seconds!

At the count of five, this brother moved with conviction to the very right side of the stage. I immediately understood what the Bible says, which I had not understood before. *"Blessed are you when people insult you, persecute you and falsely say all kinds of evil against you because of me. Rejoice and be glad, because great is your reward in heaven, for in the same way they persecuted the prophets who were before you."* Matthew 5:11-12. *"Anyone who loves their father or mother more than me is not worthy of me; anyone who loves their son or daughter more than me is not worthy of me. Whoever does not take up their cross and follow me is not worthy of me."* Matthew 10:37-38. I felt my heart warm as if a fire had been kindled in my chest. I followed my brother immediately moving to the very right side along with seven of the brothers and sisters. The faith, obedience and courage which our Lord gave to him came to me, my fear gone.

This Christian brother was arrested immediately. I never saw him again because I learned later, he died from starvation and torture. He was willing to pay the full cost of being a true disciple of Christ. The example this Christian brother gave me showed me the difference between what he did, going to the left, and where you might be a church-goer, welcomed by the crowd, never having your faith tested by trials and tribulations. The choice he made would place him in the same category as one of the great crowd of witnesses mentioned in Hebrews 12:1, *"let us throw off everything that hinders and the sin that so easily entangles. And let us run with perseverance the race marked out for us."*

The rest of us on the right were forced to stop our study and put under serious investigation. Over several years we were arrested at different times. I surprised myself when I followed the courageous steps of that brother in Christ as He took the fear from me. Three years later the Lord gave me another tough lesson to learn when I was arrested in 1960 by the secret police. I lost my freedom for 20 years. My faith and obedience were repeatedly strongly challenged in every way during the long captivity. Yet the intimacy with my Lord became stronger and deeper through these trials. I still had many ups and downs during those hard years. I still had to struggle with pain, disgrace, torture, loneliness, and discrimination. The Lord restored my faith through obedience by His special grace, mercy and miracles. My spiritual life became more mature, especially after I totally confessed my sins. My Lord never had forsaken me. Chapter 16 of *Clay in the Potter's Hand* recounts the story of my spiritual rebirth.

XXXI

Faith, Obedience and Endurance

Faith and obedience are important lessons I have had to learn. Tracing back it is clear that God has a certain plan for my life. He answered my mother's prayer precisely for me when I was yet in her womb. She gave me over to God before I was even born. The seeds of my faith began with the voice in the clouds when I was a very young child, left alone much of the time. The special circumstances of my early lonely days when my mother was so occupied with the five older stepchildren gave a strong foundation to my childlike faith. Jesus was very real to me as my "daddy" but whom I now know as my Lord and Savior. I was baptized when I was eight and a half years old. My faith in Jesus grew as my parents' example of service and their godly life showed me how to live. I wanted to follow their example and helped in as many ways as I could with the work they did in the church and other Christian organizations.

Of the nine children in our family, I was the only child who learned the real meanings of the books of ancient philosophers like Confucius, the Book of Change and Daoism. My father's influence was enormous and very special. He spent a lot of time with me teaching me how to write Chinese characters from pictures to words. These were tools he used to help me understand how to meet God. My father always explained, "Our God is not only the white man's God. He is God for all nations. He gave general revelation to all people in the world. Direct revelation was given only to His Chosen People." My father taught me the basic Biblical reason is in

Colossians 1:27 - "To them God has chosen to make known among the Gentiles the glorious riches of this mystery, which is Christ in you, the hope of glory." For the Chinese their ancient books show that God already revealed Himself in our culture. The Chinese characters for creation are an amazing example of this. They depict wind blowing through a willow branch, then a smiling mouth, soil, and a walking man. I thank God for giving me this knowledge when I was a young child.

From my childhood God prepared me for the life of a missionary. I was used to sharing my testimony both one on one and in front of a large group of people. I had done this since I was four years old. I was chosen by the teacher to be the leader of my Sunday school group even though I was so very young. I was never shy about testifying to the love of God and the truth of the Bible. From my mother I received training in music starting with piano when I was only five years old. She coached me also in singing until I was twelve years old. My voice range was extensive so I was able to sing in the choir and play the piano as well. I was able to use these gifts both in China in the house churches and when I moved to the U.S. With the use of only nine fingers, I still play the piano at Christian Aid Mission for our praise times.

My heart's desire was to become a professional opera singer, the early career my mother enjoyed. My father gave me some very sound advice about my career choice. When I was ready to choose my career, the Communists were already in power. My dream of singing Western-style operas and those hymns I loved so much were not going to be possible in the China I now lived in, my father pointed out to me. Chairman Mao was the only one I would be allowed to praise with my voice, and that I could not do. My father counseled me to enter the medical field where I could serve God by helping others. Having had three years of medical school before my studies came abruptly to a halt, I had knowledge that was very useful in my life as a missionary in later years. As God's plan for me continues to unfold, I am grateful for all of the training I have in so many different areas. My mind, my heart, my voice, and essential medical skills have all played their part in serving in the mission field.

A Bible character I can identify with is Joseph. God uses our circumstances to teach us lessons very often that can be learned no other way. My first job was as a governess to the Indonesian Ambassador's family in Beijing. When I was still at medical college, my father was arrested. With no money coming in, I had to take a position in the afternoons and evenings to support the family. While I had grown up with four servants in our home, I now found myself taking care of four very spoiled children. I was humbled by this task, as an 18 year-old, taking care of children aged seven, five, three and one. The big difference between Joseph's attitude and mine is that I complained bitterly about my situation. The lesson of humility was a hard one for me to learn. I finally stopped complaining when I realized that my Lord was also a servant. That is clear in the following Bible passage Philippians 2:6-7 *"Who, being in very nature God, did not consider equality with God something to be used to his own advantage; rather, he made himself nothing by taking the very nature of a servant, being made in human likeness."*

The lesson on endurance I learned came from my being falsely accused and sent to jail for twenty long years. This lesson is about the cost of discipleship. Carry the cross, daily deny yourself, and follow Jesus. He was the first missionary in this world. His assignment was to be the Lamb of God, spreading the Gospel, and to be crucified, to die for the sins of the whole world. His precious blood completed the redemptive work and salvation for all who accept and believe. He paid the highest price. The resurrected Jesus, our Messiah, our Savior has given us the possibility of eternal life through His sacrificial love and act of obedience to our Heavenly Father. Thank God for His glorious resurrection. In my twenty years of jail life, horrible as it was in many aspects, I started to recognize God's will was to train me to be a strong witness for Him. After I saw this, I became aware that pride was my biggest problem. I was even proud of how humble I was! John the Baptist and I learned the same lesson, that I would decrease as the Lord increased. Whenever I am weak, then I am strong. Jail was truly my theological seminary where I began to understand more fully the will of God for me.

Chapter XXXII

Miracles Abound

In Job 5:8-9 *"But if I were you, I would appeal to God; I would lay my cause before him. He performs wonders that cannot be fathomed, miracles that cannot be counted."* Patricia, William, her husband, and I prayed just before I left their home in Charlottesville for my coming trip to China in 2013. Patricia and I were working on the manuscript for this book. While this final chapter was unwritten, we thought we had the ideas all in place. God had other ideas. His plans were yet unfolding, as you will discover. He is truly a God of miracles *"that cannot be fathomed."*

This mission trip to China was one I had to undertake alone, despite my health problems. Plane trips can be very difficult with the blood clotting threat. I often have cramps in my legs as well as suffering from arthritis. As someone was probably trying to destroy our work in China, I felt I needed personally to see how bad things might be. I did not want to put anyone else at risk, especially not a coworker. At my age, if God wanted to take me home, I was more than happy to go. Being used by God for His kingdom's sake is my joy and mission. At the same time I would be delivering much needed funds to the ministries.

Our ministry in China under His power and blessing is growing very fast. With Freddie now with the Lord, I continue to work, but twice as hard. God is blessing with one miracle after another in ways unimaginable. I want to give thanks to everyone who prayed for me and cared about me during this time. Although few people knew I was going on this dangerous journey, those who did prayed mightily for my safety. God had several miracles working together in His perfect timing, beginning over a year ago, even before Freddie died.

Several days before I was to leave, I received a formal engraved invitation from the Tianjiang YWCA. I was shocked to see that I was invited to be the guest of honor to speak at the major conference celebrating the 100th anniversary of the YWCA. How did they find me? And why am I qualified to be the guest of honor? The question was answered upon my arrival. I was given the royal red carpet treatment and not hindered in any way by the authorities. Even before I deplaned, an announcement came over the loudspeaker calling my name. This was to alert me to the three people waiting to receive me as the honored guest. The result of this was my going through the customs process smoothly and given VIP treatment with a warm welcome by the YWCA staff. Only God could have arranged this miracle for my stay at a five-star hotel for four days with gorgeous meals and all the comforts one could imagine.

My mother had been the most respected president and CEO of the Tianjiang YWCA from 1936-1949. I discovered that Miss R.C. Cheng, the former General Secretary when my mother was serving as president, had personally taken credit in her papers for all that my mother had so faithfully done. This woman later became a high ranking officer in the Communist Party. My mother sought daily to fulfill the mission of the YWCA, based on John 8:32 -- *"Then you will know the truth, and the truth will set you free."* Through the friendship of Miss R.C. Cheng, the older woman, and the current General Secretary, Miss Grace Chen, they learned that I had spent my childhood in the YWCA, was still alive and living in the U.S. How did this all happen? And with such exquisite timing which is God's specialty!

Indeed, God used Miss Grace Chen, who was responsible for inviting me to be the guest speaker. She knew of my whereabouts through that "naughty boy," Winston Xu, whom she had originally asked to be the guest of honor. This mutual friend of mine since our kindergarten YWCA days in 1938-1945 knew of my charity work when he came to visit Freddie and me well over a year ago. My classmate, knowing I was not only still alive but also involved with spreading the same message that my mother had proclaimed from the beginning at the YWCA, suggested I be the guest speaker.

The audience of more than 600 people comprised not only YWCA members from many different cities, but also high ranking government officials. This 100th anniversary celebration gave me the opportunity to preach the truth of the theme of the YWCA -- You must know the Truth and the Truth will set you free. It was the same message my mother preached very often when she was the president of the YWCA before the Communists took over in 1949. It was then that Communist replaced Christian in the the YWCA title. I was able to put Christ back as I gave the message of John 8:32. The response was warm and the applause lasted a long time. Someone beside me whispered, "Thank you for your wonderful remarks. You spoke the words which we dare not speak out. You must come to visit us often!"

XXXIII

Belonging to God

Now that I am seventy-eight years old and a widow, I know that I can not please my Lord unless I am living out His will for my life. My personal character is to be loving and to share love with other people. I can be downcast at times if I do not feel loved by people. It is a very human need. God made us for love, but human love can let us down. Our selfish human nature often gets in the way and we behave in unloving ways. I have suffered through some very difficult times, and yet I am not discouraged. I know that God's will for me is to be His witness. It is my highest calling.

Freddie has finished his race. I am still here and still running, as the Lord gives me strength. He has called me to be His bride. So long as I can think, breathe, walk, and move, I am seeking His good, pleasing and perfect will. I know He has a plan still unfolding for me. I am a mother, grandmother, friend, missionary, and the Lord has claimed me as His bride, as the church is presented to Him as it says in Ephesians 5:26-27, *"holy, cleansing her by the washing with water through the word, and to present her to himself as a radiant church, without stain or wrinkle or any other blemish, but holy and blameless."*

No one knows when the day will come when we will be called home. We need to be ready and alert. I want to have the oil in my lamp, to stay strong and to be prepared like the wise maidens. Every sin we might commit has already been forgiven, but Satan never stops attacking the faith and body of God's people. I want to be holy, set apart from this world. I know we have to live in the world, as I continue to go on my way rejoicing and spreading God's love, for it is His love and faithfulness upon which I can rely. Lord, Your kingdom is forever. He has set a seal upon my heart and my arms. I am His and He is mine.

Three songs are particularly meaningful to me and I hope they will bless you as well. With my reborn voice I very often praise my Lord as I sing these songs: "Embrace the Cross," "My Tribute," and "We Shall Behold Him." With permission, I share the lyrics with you.

This first song is very often how I close after preaching at churches and conferences. It is dear to my heart.

Embrace the Cross
by John G. Elliott
I am crucified with Christ
Therefore I no longer live
Jesus Christ now lives in me
(repeat twice)
    Embrace the cross
    Where Jesus suffered
    Though it will cost
    All you claim as yours
    Your sacrifice will seem small
    Beside the treasure
    Eternity can't measure
    What Jesus holds in store
        Embrace the love
        The cross requires
        Cling to the one
        Whose heart knew every pain
        Receive from Jesus
        Fountains of compassion
        Your heart to move as His
        Oh, wondrous cross our desires rest in you
        Lord Jesus make us bolder
        To face with courage the shame and disgrace
        You bore upon your shoulder
            Embrace the life
            That comes from dying
            Come trace the steps
            The Savior walked for you

An empty tomb
Concludes Golgotha's sorrow
Endure then till tomorrow
Your cross of suffering
Embrace the cross
Embrace the cross
Embrace the cross of Jesus

—With permission - License No. 557519

The second song was written by Andraé Crouch and the words express exactly how I feel --- To God Be the Glory.

My Tribute
How can I say thanks for the things
You have done for me?
Things so undeserved yet You gave
To prove your love for me
The voices of a million angels
Could not express my gratitude
All that I am, and ever hope to be
I owe it all to thee
   To God be the glory, to God be the glory
   To God be the glory for the things He has done
   With His blood He has saved me
   With His power He has raised me
To God be the glory for the things He has done
   Just let me live my life and
   Let it be pleasing Lord to thee
   And if I gain any praise, let it go to Calvary
   With His blood He has saved me
   With His power He has raised me
   To God be the glory for the things He has done

—With permission - License No. 557449

The final song I want to share with you was written by the late Dottie Rambo.

We Shall Behold Him
The sky shall unfold, preparing His entrance;
the stars shall applaud Him with thunders of praise.
The sweet light in His eyes shall enhance those awaiting,
and we shall behold Him, face to face.
Chorus
We shall behold Him.
Yes, we shall behold Him,
face to face in all of His glory
We shall behold Him.
Yes, we shall behold Him,
face to face, our Savior and Lord.
The angels shall sound the shout of His coming,
the sleeping shall rise from their slumbering place.
And those who remain shall be changed in a moment,
and we shall behold Him then face to face.
—With permission - License No. 557520

Beginnings

My parents, left, mother Miriam Nieh, and right, father David Chang

Left, my nanny

Right, started to learn to serve

In the kindergarten of the church, I am the one in the center of the first row in white clothes

Left, my naughty brother Joe was squeezing my shoulder while taking this photo.

Right, raising support for YWCA with my mother

Above and at right, Our first wedding day

When I was young

When my twin sons were eight years old

Christian Aid Mission

Dr. Bob and Cynthia Finley (founder and President of Christian Aid)

Started full time serving the Lord with Christian Aid as a missionary, 1987

Ordained as a missionary by Dr. Bob Finley and Jeffery Shaw, at the beginning of my ministry at Christian Aid, 1988

Freddie and I attended Lausanne in Holland in 2000

Dr. Finley preaching to Chinese student scholars

Revival Chinese Christian Church retreat conference

Dr. Finley baptizing more than 50 Chinese scholars

Many Chinese scholars come to Christ

Chinese New Year

Our 30th wedding anniversary

Celebrated our 20th wedding anniversary at Reedy Creek Baptist Church

Celebrated our 25th wedding anniversary at Christian Aid Mission

Christian Aid China Division helped with Chinese Christian weddings

Left, being an interpreter for foreign visitors

My baby sister, Grace

China

Serving Chinese tribal churches in Yunnan province, China

Telling the story of Jesus to Tibetans in China

Serving Chinese tribal house churches in Xingjiang province, China

Discipling tribal teachers in China

Serving Chinese tribal house churches in the mountains of China

Orphan children salute dear donors with me in China

Taiwan

Standing with Allen Hau at the Taiwan CCEA World Mission department

Preaching at the Taiwanese Legislature Christian Fellowship

I was able to preach with criminals at the Taiwan jail

President of World Vision Taiwan, Dr. Hank Du and Mrs. Du

Rev James and Mrs. Shia, President of Chinese Christian Evangelical Association, Taiwan

Sharing with elders about Israel Chinese Ministry

Left, Dorothy started Chinese Ministry for Israel

Dorothy is a consultant for the Global Gospel Cinese Characters Association

Dorothy met with the leaders of the Stock, Bank, Insurance Companies Christian Fellowship

Nicknamed "Fireball," Dorothy preaches with deep emotion as she tells about the Lord's work in her life

Dorothy sharing more after worship services

Speaking at the Taiwan Assembly of God

Mission Trips

Preaching in Australia Chinese churches

The Christian Aid office in Brazil Philippines

Singapore

Puerto Rico

I spoke at Women's Aglow 25th anniversary conference in Canada

Philippines

Music

Choir reunion at "Remembering the Good Old Days" Chinese Christian conference in Canada

Singing solo part in Messiah concert in ChapelHill, NC in 1984

Violinist Mary Frances Boyce (l) and vocalist Mrs Peacock (r)

With nine fingers (the tenth has no feeling) and a reborn voice, God still uses me in worshipping

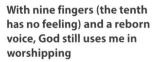

Friends

Dr. Rev. David Jeremiah

Dr. Rev Thomas Wang, Founder and President of The Great Commission Center International

Miss Daisy Li and Martha Kang

Dr. Joseph Lam (Founder and President of World Children's Fund)

Dr. Steve and Mrs. Dennie Chang and Grace Chang are our great helpers

Mr. and Mrs. Windsor (childhood friends)

Family

My son Daniel, daughter-in-law Julia, and grandchildren

My son Joseph, daughter-in-law Rebecca, and grandchildren

My chief editor, mind reader, soul mate and sweet gifted sister-in-Christ, Patricia Taylor